W9-CEO-979

DISCARD

DISCARD

PEOPLE
to
KNOW
TODAY

LAURA BUSH

Portrait of a First Lady

Laura B. Edge

NEW YORK MILLS
PUBLIC LIBRARY
399 MAIN STREET
N.Y. MILLS, NY 13417

DISCARD

Enslow Publishers, Inc.
40 Industrial Road
Box 398
Berkeley Heights, NJ 07922
USA
http://www.enslow.com

Copyright © 2006 by Laura B. Edge

All rights reserved.

No part of this book may be reproduced by any means
without the written permission of the publisher.

Library of Congress Cataloging-in-Publication Data

Edge, Laura Bufano, 1953–
   Laura Bush : portrait of a First Lady / by Laura Edge.
      p. cm. — (People to know today)
   Includes bibliographical references and index.
   ISBN 0-7660-2629-9
   1. Bush, Laura Welch, 1946– .—Juvenile literature. 2. Presidents' spouses—United
States—Biography—Juvenile literature. I. Title. II. Series.
   E904.B87E34 2005
   973.931092–dc22

                        2005034883

Printed in the United States of America

10 9 8 7 6 5 4 3 2 1

To Our Readers: We have done our best to make sure all Internet Addresses in this book were
active and appropriate when we went to press. However, the author and the publisher have no
control over and assume no liability for the material available on those Internet sites or on
other Web sites they may link to. Any comments or suggestions can be sent by e-mail to
comments@enslow.com or to the address on the back cover.

Every effort has been made to locate all copyright holders of material used in this book. If any
errors or omissions have occurred, corrections will be made in future editions of this book.

Illustration Credits: Photo Credits: © Southern Methodist University, Photo by
Hillsman S. Jackson, p. 24; AP/Wide World, pp. 1, 4, 7, 10, 29, 38, 53, 55, 57, 61,
64, 69, 75, 78, 81, 82, 88, 94, 98, 100, 103, 107, 109; classmates.com, p. 19;
Enslow Publishers, Inc., p. 16; George Bush Presidential Library, pp. 34, 36, 40, 41,
45, 46, 49, 50; Getty Images, p. 91; Paul J. Richards/AFP/Getty Images, p. 71.

Cover Photograph: Getty Images

CONTENTS

Laura Bush

1
THE NATIONAL
BOOK FESTIVAL

On Saturday morning, September 8, 2001, First Lady Laura Bush and Dr. James Billington stood in front of the Library of Congress in Washington, D.C. Against a colorful backdrop of balloons, banners, and a brilliant blue sky, they opened the first National Book Festival. Dr. Billington, the Librarian of Congress, introduced Laura Bush as "the first professional librarian ever to live in the White House."[1] Laura Bush thanked the volunteers who had turned her idea for the festival into a reality. Then she welcomed the crowd. "We're all in for a treat at this festival," she said.[2]

Laura Bush had planned the National Book Festival with Dr. Billington to celebrate America's authors and to raise awareness of reading and literacy. Reading had always been an important part of her life. As a child, Bush read piles of good books. As a teacher and librarian, she read to her students and helped them develop a love of reading. As first lady of Texas, she used her position to encourage literacy. She founded the Texas Book Festival, a highly successful event enjoyed by thousands of Texans each year.

With the National Book Festival, Laura Bush brought her vision for literacy to the national stage. By sharing her love of books, she hoped more families would make reading a central part of their lives. "This event gives us an opportunity to inspire parents and care givers to read to children as early as possible and to encourage reading as a lifelong activity," she said.[3]

Festival events were held in the Library of Congress and in six huge white tents on the east lawn of the U.S. Capitol. There were special areas for children and young adults, fiction and imagination, history and current events, and mystery and suspense. Thousands of guests from

With the National Book Festival, Laura Bush brought her vision for literacy to the national stage.

the Washington, D.C., area, as well as across the country, enjoyed meeting authors, illustrators, and storytellers. They listened to their favorite authors read from their books and talk about the inspiration behind

The first lady handed out free books at the National Book Festival.

them. Guests also bought autographed copies to take home.

Surrounded by Secret Service agents, Laura Bush strolled from tent to tent and mingled with festival guests. She chatted with children and watched them pose for pictures with Clifford the Big Red Dog and Arthur. In the children's area, author Richard Peck read from his Newbery Award–winning middle-grade novel, *A Year Down Yonder*. Nonfiction author Russell Freedman, who prefers to be called a "factual author," talked about how some people think nonfiction books are not as interesting as fiction books. He tries to stamp out that myth with every book he writes.

Laura Bush strolled from tent to tent and mingled with festival guests.

When Laura Bush planned the festival, she made sure it included something for everyone. Ord, the blue dragon from the PBS series *Dragon Tales*, met fans on the Capitol lawn. A few of Laura Bush's favorite children's book characters also joined in the fun. Wilbur and Charlotte from *Charlotte's Web*, the cat from *The Cat in the Hat*, and Peter Rabbit surprised and delighted the youngest festival guests.

For teens, Laura Bush invited National Basketball Association players to take part in the festival. "We're here to launch our Read to Achieve program," basketball player Michael Curry told the crowd, "and to show you the importance of education; even professional basketball players can't have a career without an education."[4] In the young adult pavilion, teens listened to NBA players talk about their favorite books. "One book can change your perspective," said basketball player Theo Ratliff.[5]

In the young adult pavilion, teens listened to NBA players talk about their favorite books.

On the Neptune Plaza, festival guests enjoyed a wide variety of musical performances. They heard Appalachian folk music, Scottish and Irish music and dance, the Mariachi Los Amigos band, and a Dixieland Band. At the storytelling pavilion, dozens of baby strollers could be seen parked outside the tent. Inside, festival guests heard stories by Navajo Indians who had worked as code talkers in World War II. They told how they sent messages for the Marines in their native language in a secret code that was never broken by the enemy. Children watched hand puppets from Taiwan and dancers from India.

In addition to bringing readers together with their favorite writers, Laura Bush planned the festival as a way to show off the Library of Congress. In the Thomas Jefferson Building, with its white Italian marble, twenty-three-karat gold leaf ceiling, and stained glass, festival guests were treated to special

Library of Congress

The Library of Congress is the largest library in the world. It contains more than 130 million items on approximately 530 miles of bookshelves. The collections include more than 29 million books and other printed materials, 2.7 million recordings, 12 million photographs, 4.8 million maps, and 58 million manuscripts. Each of the three buildings of the library was named after a president of the United States who helped create the library: Thomas Jefferson, John Adams, and James Madison. The library is the research division for Congress and has helped thousands of people find the facts they need.

tours. Specialists from the conservation division offered advice on the best way to care for books, scrapbooks, family albums, and photographs. The reading rooms showed the art of writing in the languages and scripts of the world.

In the Madison Building, festival guests competed in a trivia contest about America's first ladies. They also learned how to use the library's online research tools and how to register books, poetry, and music with the copyright office of the United States government.

Visitors to the National Book Festival were invited to tour the Library of Congress.

More than twenty-five thousand people went to the first National Book Festival. For those who could not attend, C-SPAN 2 filmed many of the events and showed them on an eight-hour television program the following day. The first festival was such a huge success, it has become an annual event.

Laura Bush has spent her life talking to children about reading. For years, she did it one child at a time. As her influence grew, she expanded to larger and larger audiences. "I love to read, and I want more Americans to experience the sense of adventure and satisfaction that comes from reading a good book," she said.[6]

Laura Bush has turned her passion for books into a quest for world literacy. With the creation of the National Book Festival, she has shared her vision with thousands of people. Three days after the festival, on September 11, 2001, the United States was attacked by terrorists. Laura Bush enlarged her role as first lady and helped comfort the nation. From her simple beginnings in the heart of West Texas, that was quite an accomplishment.

2
WEST TEXAS GIRL

Laura's father, Harold Bruce Welch, had grown up in Lubbock, Texas. The son of a builder, Harold watched his father and dreamed of building homes himself one day. When World War II broke out, Harold fought with the United States Army in Germany. In 1944, he came home on leave and married Jenna Louise Hawkins.

Jenna was the only child of Arkansas farmers. Her family moved to El Paso, Texas, when she was a baby. Jenna's mother taught her to love nature. Jenna spent her childhood studying the birds, trees, and wildflowers of West Texas.

After the war ended, Harold and Jenna lived in El Paso for a few months. In May 1946, they moved to the growing town of Midland, Texas. Located halfway between Fort Worth and El Paso on the flat West Texas plain, Midland began as a cattle shipping town. Hot, dry, and dusty, Midland was a land of sandstorms and tumbleweeds, rattlesnakes and scorpions. Then oil was discovered in the area, and Midland became the business center for oil companies in West Texas. Its population doubled. Harold Welch saw an opportunity to design and build homes for the steady stream of families moving to the Midland area. He was working as a district manager for a company that gave loans to car buyers. In his spare time he learned the construction business.

Harold and Jenna Welch also picked Midland because they wanted a large family. Jenna was pregnant again, after suffering several miscarriages. She and Harold thought Midland would be a safe place to raise children. Midland was a small town, a place of family and community. Children played in the streets until twilight and skipped home to unlocked doors. Neighbors looked out for one another, and the town had very little crime.

Laura Lane Welch was born on November 4, 1946. She was named for her grandmothers, Jessie Laura Hawkins and Marie Lula Lane Welch. Jenna and Harold Welch were thrilled to finally have a healthy child. They adored their daughter. Laura was an easy baby. "She never cried and she was hardly ever sick," said her mother.[1]

Jenna read to her daughter from the time she was an infant. Laura cherished those moments curled up beside her mother listening to stories. Like most women of her generation, Laura's mother was a traditional housewife. She took care of Laura, cooked three meals a day, and managed the household. Jenna Welch was also an avid reader. She enjoyed bird-watching and identifying the wildflowers of West Texas. Harold Welch was a fun-loving dad who liked to laugh. He rushed home from work each night to play with his daughter.

In 1950, Harold Welch's dream came true. He became a home builder. He quit his job with the credit company and formed a building company with Lloyd Waynick, a local contractor. Waynick and Welch Builders built more than two hundred homes in Midland. Laura enjoyed watching her father build homes. "It was very satisfying to be able to drive down the street and see what he'd done," she said.[2] While her father built houses, Laura's mother did the bookkeeping for the company.

Laura started kindergarten in 1951. As a five-year-old, she studied ballet and took swimming lessons at the public pool in Hogan Park. She

A New Boy In Town

In March 1950, George Herbert Walker Bush, his wife, Barbara; their three-year-old son, George W.; and infant daughter, Robin, moved to Midland. They bought a house not far from the Welch home on Easter Egg Row. The neighborhood got its name because each identical house was painted the color of an Easter egg: red, blue, green, and pink. The two families did not meet until the 1970s.

also joined the children's choir at the First Methodist Church.

The Welches loved animals. Their dog, a terrier named Bully, became Laura's constant companion. Laura also had pet cats. She received a tabby from her friend Judy Jones Ryan, who later said that the cat "had a real pug nose, kind of flat, and she would always push on his nose. It was a tabby. And she loved it and always loved cats from then on."[3]

In second grade Laura walked to James Bowie Elementary School. She often had to wipe off her desk before class to clean away the dust from sandstorms. She was a good student, made friends easily, and enjoyed school.

Inspired by her second-grade teacher, Charlene Gnagy, Laura decided to become a teacher. She loved to play school and practiced teaching on her dolls. Once, she and a friend set up classrooms in two bedrooms of Laura's house. The girls lined the dolls up in rows. Then they stepped out of the room to talk. Laura's mother asked why they were chatting in the hallway instead of teaching their classes. Laura replied, "Well, that's what our teachers do."[4]

> **Laura was a good student, made friends easily, and enjoyed school.**

Laura's favorite childhood activity was reading, a passion she shared with her mother. She spent hours

As a child, Laura loved to read.

lost in exciting worlds hidden in the pages of books. Her favorites were the *Little House* books by Laura Ingalls Wilder and *The Secret Garden* by Frances Hodgson Burnett.

Reading introduced Laura to families of all sizes. She longed for brothers and sisters. Her parents wanted more children too, but were not able to have any more. Laura tried to be the best daughter in the world to make them happy. "I felt very obligated to my parents," she said. "I didn't want to upset them in any way."[5]

Once a week, Laura and her friends wore their Brownie uniforms to school and walked to a troop meeting after school. The girls made crafts and ate cookies. Laura enjoyed the friendships she made in Brownies. She also liked the activities. A careful worker, she took her time and was creative and artistic.

When Laura was eight years old, she moved up from Brownies to Girl Scouts. Her mother became the Scout leader. Jenna Welch taught the girls how to identify the colorful array of Texas birds. Laura and her friends earned their bird-watching badges.

As a Girl Scout, Laura attended her first summer camp. The camp sat in a beautiful valley in the Davis Mountains, two hundred miles southwest of Midland. Coyotes, wild turkeys, deer, and jackrabbits lived in the wilderness around the camp. But Laura grew homesick and asked to go home after one week. Jenna and Harold Welch drove to camp and brought their daughter home.

In the fall of 1958, Laura entered seventh grade at San Jacinto Junior High. The school was much larger than her elementary school. Laura knew many of her classmates from James Bowie and made the transition easily. Some of the students in her new school had attended a private elementary school. They did not know their public school classmates. Laura did her best to make the new students feel welcome. She invited them to join in school activities. George W. Bush also attended San Jacinto Junior High for one year. Then his family moved to Houston, Texas.

In seventh grade, Laura decided where she wanted to go to college. A book helped her make the choice. She read a biography of football star Doak Walker, who had played football for Southern Methodist University in Dallas, Texas. He was named All-American three years in a row and won the Heisman Trophy in 1948. In addition to his athletic skills, Walker had a reputation for being a great role model and an all-around nice guy. Laura admired Walker and wanted to go to the same college. "From that point forward, I wanted to attend SMU," she said.[6]

Summer temperatures in Midland can climb into the 100s. Laura and her friends spent the long summer days at the city swimming pool. Afterward, they often hopped on their bikes and pedaled over to Laura's house. Her friends felt welcome at the Welch home. They sat around the kitchen table, drank sodas, and chatted with her parents. Laura's house became a popular hangout.

Laura's friends often slept over at her house. The girls read Louisa May Alcott's classic novel *Little Women.* "I still see us propped up in a big double bed, eating crackers, while we read and reread Beth's death," said her childhood friend Georgia Todd Temple.[7] The crackers always wound up soggy from the girls' tears.

Laura's house became a popular hangout.

In 1961, Laura started tenth grade at the brand-new Robert E. Lee High School. She took honors classes and worked on the yearbook, *RebeLee.* She also joined the YMCA's Tri-Hi-Y, a social service club for teenage girls. Tri-Hi-Y taught the teens to be leaders. They looked for ways to serve their community and make it better. They visited nursing homes, volunteered on teacher appreciation day, and cleaned up the school grounds.

Friday nights were football nights in Midland. Dressed in the school colors of maroon and white, Laura and her friends piled into the family car and headed to the football stadium. After cheering for their team, the Rebels, the girls cruised around town or stopped at the diner for hamburgers and cherry cokes. They often ended up at Laura's house for a slumber party where they listened to the Beatles and danced around in their socks. Laura had a keen sense of humor and liked to tease. One of her high school friends later called her "very outgoing, with a little mischievous streak."[8]

During the summer between tenth and eleventh grades, Laura and a group of classmates traveled to Monterrey, Mexico. For six weeks, they attended Spanish language and culture classes during the day. They also toured Monterrey's historic churches and

In high school, Laura was "very outgoing, with a little mischievous streak," according to a friend.

Laura had a keen sense of humor and liked to tease.

shopped at open-air markets. At night, the girls listened to Mexican pop music on the radio and tried to translate the lyrics into English.

Laura had a positive outlook on life. "She never complained," said her high school friend Peggy Porter Weiss.[9] Once, Peggy stopped by Laura's house and found Laura in the backyard. Laura was picking the ticks off her dog Marty and placing them in a jar. A squeamish Peggy admitted she would never do that, and if someone forced her to, she would complain the whole time. Laura kept looking for tics and said, "It's not so bad."[10]

On November 6, 1963, two days after her seventeenth birthday, Laura and her friend Judy Dykes were on their way to a party. Laura drove through a stop sign and accidently hit a 1962 Corvair. Laura and Judy suffered only a few scratches and bruises. The driver of the Corvair, Michael Douglas, was killed in the crash. Michael, a high school track star, was a friend of Laura's.

"Laura's accident had a huge impact on the town," said Midland resident Robert McCleskey. "Everybody knew about it and everybody was shaken up."[11] Laura was not charged or ticketed in the accident. She grieved over the loss of her friend and struggled with the fact that she had caused the crash and Michael's death. She met with her pastor for counseling at First Methodist

Church. She stayed home from school for a few weeks, unable to talk to her friends. "I grieved a lot," she said. "It was a horrible, horrible tragedy. It's a terrible feeling to be responsible for an accident."[12]

As Laura wrestled with her personal grief, another tragedy in Texas gripped the nation two weeks later. On November 22, 1963, President John F. Kennedy was shot and killed in Dallas. Laura's emotions were still raw after Michael's death. She was stunned by President Kennedy's assassination.

November 1963 was a turning point in Laura's life. She learned that life carries pain as well as joy and that death is a part of life. When she returned to school, she wrote a tribute to Michael Douglas for the yearbook. As Laura finished out her senior year, she never talked about the accident, but it deeply affected her and she quietly grieved.

> "I grieved a lot. . . . It's a terrible feeling to be responsible for an accident."

3
TEACHER AND LIBRARIAN

In September 1964, Laura Welch started college at Southern Methodist University (SMU) in Dallas, Texas. SMU, a conservative, private university, sat in a wealthy section of Dallas. The campus had tree-shaded lawns and plentiful flower beds. Brick buildings dotted the quiet landscape. Welch and the other female students wore skirts or dresses to class, and students were held to a 10 P.M. curfew. Sheltered on the SMU campus, Laura Welch's college experience did not include the drug use, race riots, and Vietnam War protests that took place on so many college campuses in the 1960s. "My generation was just right on the cusp," she said. "It was a fairly conservative campus compared with how it was just a few years after that for the little brothers and sisters of my friends."[1]

Laura Welch had decided in second grade to become a teacher. She majored in elementary education at SMU. "I think teachers have a more profound impact on our society and culture than any other profession," she said.[2] Welch enjoyed her classes, especially English and children's literature. She also discovered the work of Russian novelist Fyodor Dostoyevski. His novel *The Brothers Karamazov* became her favorite book.

Harold Welch had been saving for his daughter's college education since she was in first grade, so Laura Welch did not need to work to earn money for school. She studied hard and had an active social life. She also spent hours lounging by the pool. She listened to her favorite band, the Beatles, and played bridge. She joined the Kappa Alpha Theta sorority and moved into the sorority house. Her room was "always the central headquarters for fun," said sorority sister Susan Nowlin. "She was never one to tell people, 'I have to study, so everyone has to leave.'"[3]

One night, Laura Welch and a group of friends were hanging out in Welch's room. She suddenly hopped up and pretended to wave to a crowd of admirers. Asked what she was doing, she drawled, "I need to practice my Miss America wave. You just never know when it will come in handy."[4]

Several of Welch's high school friends also attended SMU. Sometimes the girls' mothers would drive up to Dallas and take their daughters shopping. They shopped at pricey stores not found in Midland.

Laura Welch was popular in college and dated many different young men. "Laura always had a boyfriend—some good-looking guy to go out with," said one of her Midland friends. "But she would never allow herself to get serious about anyone."[5]

Laura Welch often returned to Midland on weekends to visit her parents and friends. On one visit, she attended the Minuet Club Debutante Ball. She wore a floor-length white satin gown and elbow-length gloves. She carried a bouquet of roses. At the debutante ball, Welch and her friends were presented to society, a tradition that dates back to the royal courts of England.

Welch spent her summers in Midland with her parents. She taught swimming for the City of Midland.

Laura went to college at Southern Methodist University.

She also camped at Bandera, Texas, the Cowboy Capitol of the World. Welch and her mother often took trips to El Paso or Lubbock to visit her grandparents. She and her mother took turns driving and reading to each other. They read all kinds of books, from popular novels to the classics.

The summer between her junior and senior year of college, Laura Welch was a camp counselor at Camp Mystic on the Guadalupe River in the Texas Hill country. She enjoyed working with the children, being outdoors, and earning her own money.

By her senior year of college, Welch wore peasant skirts, tie-dyed blouses, and bell-bottoms like the rest of her classmates. Feminism and women's liberation were new terms being discussed on college campuses at the time. Welch read books on the roles of women in society and thought about women's issues. She believed in equality for everyone and thought women should be paid the same as men for doing the same jobs. Once, she even challenged her dad. She told him he had "programmed" her to be a teacher, a traditional job for women, instead of a doctor or a lawyer. Her dad laughed, pulled out his wallet, and said, "I'll send you to law school."[6] When he did that, Welch admitted she did not want to be a lawyer. She wanted to be a teacher.

Laura Welch graduated from SMU in 1968. After graduation, she wanted to backpack through Europe with a group of college friends. Her parents were not comfortable with that plan, but they did want their daughter to travel overseas and expand her horizons. They arranged for her to go to Europe with her uncle Mark Welch, his wife, and their teenage daughter Mary. The group visited London, Paris, and Rome. For Laura, "it was a magical experience. It made all the things I'd read about in books come alive."[7]

At the end of the summer in 1968, school started and Laura Welch did not have a job. All the teaching positions in Dallas were filled. She went to work in a Dallas insurance office, hoping a teaching position would open up soon. A few months later, she got a call from a Dallas public school. She jumped at the chance to teach third grade.

> "It was a **magical experience.** It made all the things I'd **read** about in books come **alive.**"

Welch soon discovered that many of her students could not read. She worked with them to improve their reading skills, but her favorite part of the job was reading to them. She tried to bring the characters in books to life for her students. When she found a spider web in the corner of her classroom, she saved it for Charlotte, the spider in E. B. White's classic children's book *Charlotte's Web*.

In 1969, Laura Welch moved to Houston and took a job as a second-grade teacher at John F. Kennedy Elementary School. The school was in a poor, mostly African-American district. "I think teaching in minority schools opened my eyes," she said. "It made me realize how unfair in a lot of ways life is."[8] Welch enjoyed teaching and working with children. "I think mainly I just learned about the dignity of every human, and every child, and how important every single child is and how important each one of their lives are," she said.[9]

Welch was a popular teacher. "The kids really did love her," said Larry Gatson, one of her second-grade students. "She'd go outside and play with us. If you had problems on reading and spelling, she'd take a little more time with you."[10] At the end of the school year, Welch had grown so attached to her students that she asked to move up with them to third grade. Her principal agreed and she taught the same group of students the following year. "I felt very close to them," she said.[11]

Welch lived in Houston's most popular singles apartment complex, the Chateaux Dijon. She shared the apartment with a friend from Midland, Jan Donnelly. This apartment complex for young people had a rowdy side, where the residents threw parties, played volleyball in one of six pools, and held belly flop contests. It also had a quiet side, for the less party-minded residents. Laura Welch lived on the quiet side. A young man from Midland, George W. Bush, lived on the noisy side of the apartment complex. The two never met.

After teaching for two years in Houston, Welch became convinced that reading was the key to all learning. If she could teach her students to become strong readers, they could learn any subject. She decided to focus all her energies on teaching children to read. "A love of reading does not automatically translate into the ability to teach a child to read," she said. "Even with a degree in education and practice as a student teacher, I wasn't totally prepared for teaching reading. I took pride in my educational training, but the job was much harder than I had imagined."[12] She decided to go back to college.

In 1971, she enrolled in a master's program at the University of Texas at Austin, where she studied to become a librarian. She attended classes to help her evaluate books for children and offer reading guidance. She also learned the history of libraries, cataloging, and classification and earned a master's degree in library science in 1973.

After graduation, Welch moved back to Houston and accepted a job as a children's librarian at the McCrane-Kashmere Gardens Public Library. She chose the downtown library as a good place to meet single men. "I didn't have the opportunity to meet that many men to date," she said, "and I thought by working in a big public library in downtown Houston, I might have a different social life."[13]

Welch found she missed the elementary school

Laura Welsh hoped that working in downtown Houston would boost her social life.

setting. She moved back to Austin in 1974 and took a job as school librarian at Mollie Dawson Elementary School. Most of the students at the school were Hispanic. Welch's knowledge of the Spanish language came in handy in her new job. She loved reading to her students. She became an expert at reading upside down so she could show the pictures as she read.

She taught reading comprehension as she read stories. She told the children to think about how the characters felt and to imagine what they were thinking. She often stopped and asked her students what they thought would happen next in the story. Welch was passionate about teaching children to read. She wanted each of them to share her love of books. She also helped the older students learn how to do research.

Laura Welch was happy with her job. "I made my love of books my career," she said.[14] She often went out on Friday nights for Mexican food with her fellow teachers. Welch's favorites were enchiladas and tacos. The young women relaxed, chatted about the week, and munched on chips and salsa.

Welch continued to date, but there was still no one she wanted to get serious about. She often drove home to Midland on the weekends to visit with her parents and old friends. On one of those trips Welch met the man who would change her life.

4

A PERFECT MATCH

Laura Welch was thirty years old in the summer of 1977. Most of her friends were married, but Welch did not seem in any hurry to become a bride. When the right person came along, she would get married and have children. But for now, she was content. She had a job she loved, lots of friends, and an active social life.

Sometimes, Welch's friends tried to introduce her to eligible bachelors. Jan Donnelly, Welch's former roommate in Houston, was one of those matchmakers. Donnelly had married Joe O'Neill and lived in Midland. Welch often visited the couple on her frequent trips home. The O'Neills wanted to introduce Jan's friend Laura Welch to Joe's friend George W. Bush.

George Bush and Joe O'Neill had grown up together

in Midland. As children, they rode bikes and played baseball together. As young adults, they both worked in the oil business and cheered the Midland Angels, a minor league baseball team. Laura Welch did not know George Bush personally, but she knew of the Bush family. The elder George Bush and Barbara Bush were active in the Midland community and well known to most residents.

The first time Jan O'Neill invited Laura Welch to meet George W. Bush, Welch declined. "I thought he was someone real political, and I wasn't interested," she said.[1] Bush had recently announced he was running for Congress. Politics was an important part of the Bush family tradition. George W's great-great-great-uncle on his mother's side was President Franklin Pierce. His grandfather Prescott Bush served as senator from Connecticut. His father, George H.W. Bush, had recently served in the House of Representatives.

The O'Neills did not give up. In August 1977, they invited Laura and George to a backyard barbecue. This time, Laura Welch said yes. After they were introduced, George Bush talked nonstop. Laura Welch listened. Jan O'Neill was thrilled with her matchmaking skills, noting that Bush, who usually went home by

> Laura Welch did not **know** George Bush **personally,** but she knew of the Bush **family.**

nine o'clock, stayed until midnight. Laura Welch and George Bush played miniature golf with the O'Neills the following night. Bush drove to Austin the following weekend to see Welch. "When we met, I was enthralled," said Bush. "I found her to be a very thoughtful, smart, interested person—one of the great listeners. And since I'm one of the big talkers, it was a great fit."[2]

Shortly after meeting Laura Welch, Bush flew to Kennebunkport, Maine, for the annual Bush family vacation. His parents were surprised when he called Welch several times from Maine. Welch rarely answered the phone. When she did, she told Bush she was busy and would try to call him back. George's mother, Barbara Bush, knew her son had met someone special when he cut his vacation short and flew back to Austin to see Laura Welch. "He was struck by lightning when he met her," she said.[3]

George Bush drove to Austin nearly every weekend to see Laura Welch. Jenna Welch, Laura's mother, worried that George would push Laura away with his nonstop attention."I was afraid George was going to ruin the whole thing because he was rushing it," she said. "In the past, when Laura brought home these nice young men from SMU, that had turned her off."[4]

The match surprised many of Laura Welch's friends. She was quiet and reserved. George Bush was loud and outgoing. She enjoyed staying home curled

Laura and George hit it off immediately.

up with a good book. He enjoyed being around people and was usually the life of the party. In spite of their different personalities, Laura Welch and George Bush fell in love. "We quickly realized that they were perfect complements to one another," said Regan Gammon, Welch's best friend since third grade. "Laura loved George's energy, and George loved the way she was so calm."[5]

George Bush described Laura Welch as, "gorgeous,

good-humored, quick to laugh, down-to-earth, and very smart."[6] She said of Bush, "He adds a lot of excitement to my life. I think that's one of the reasons I was attracted to him. He was high-energy and fun and had a great sense of humor."[7] A few months after they met, they began planning their wedding.

In October 1977, George Bush took Laura Welch to Houston to meet his parents. When the couple walked through the front door, George's brother Jeb greeted them. Jeb dropped down on one knee before Laura Welch. "Did you pop the question to her, George, old boy?" asked Jeb. While George turned red, Laura answered for him. "Yes, as a matter of fact he has, and I accepted," she said.[8]

> **"Laura loved George's energy, and George loved the way she was so calm."**

George's brothers and sister cheered. His parents were surprised. "We didn't even know he wanted to get married until he showed up at the door with this beautiful creature, Laura, and announced that she was going to be his wife," said Barbara Bush.[9]

A few weeks later, Bush and Welch traveled to Kennebunkport, Maine, so he could introduce her to the rest of his family. Welch felt at home at the rowdy Bush compound. She had always wanted a large family and enjoyed being included in the Bush clan. "She has an extremely gracious and gentle way about

George invited Laura to spend weekends in Maine with his family.

her that brings peace to a place that could otherwise be chaotic," said George's brother Marvin. "The doors were always slamming, everybody was running around and playing sports in an extremely male-oriented family. Laura was an only child—but she fit in beautifully."[10]

On Bush family vacations, the sports-minded family often played baseball, tennis, and golf. They sailed boats. They loved physical activity and fierce competition. George Bush's grandmother, Dorothy

Walker Bush, wanted to find out what sports Laura Welch played. When the two women met, Dorothy Bush asked, "What do you do?"

"I read," replied Laura Welch.[11] It was clearly not the answer Dorothy Bush expected.

When Laura Welch and George Bush returned to Midland, they went out to dinner with her parents, Harold and Jenna Welch. Bush asked Harold Welch for his daughter's hand in marriage, and Welch gave his consent.

Laura Welch and George W. Bush were married on November 5, 1977, in the Glass Chapel of the First United Methodist Church in Midland. The bride wore a street-length beige dress with a single strand of white pearls. She wore a corsage of white gardenias at her waist. The wedding took place the day after Welch's thirty-first birthday. George Bush was also thirty-one years old. Seventy-five friends and family members attended the simple ceremony. The couple

Just Like Mom and Dad

Laura Welch saw several traits in George Bush that she admired in her father. "My daddy loved to laugh," she said. "He was funny and didn't take himself too seriously. Also, both my dad and George tried to make people feel good."[12] Several of Laura Welch's friends noticed the similarity between George and Laura and Harold and Jenna Welch. "George and Laura are not unlike Harold and Jenna," said Robert McCleskey, who had known them all since childhood. "Mrs. Welch was the quiet Sunday School teacher, Harold was the fun-loving type of guy who talked up a storm."[13]

The couple posed for a wedding day photo with his parents,
President and Mrs. Bush.

honeymooned in Mexico. Laura quit her job as a school librarian in Austin and moved into George's brick ranch house in Midland.

The couple did not stay in Midland for long. They loaded up George Bush's white Oldsmobile and hit the campaign trail. The newlyweds spent the first year of their marriage driving around West Texas while George Bush campaigned for Congress. "I worried about the stress of the political campaign combined with the stress of being newlyweds," said Laura Bush.[14] But since George Bush promised his new bride she would not have to give political speeches, she relaxed and enjoyed herself. "We were never mad at each other because we always had opponents," she said, adding that it was "a great way to spend a honeymoon."[15]

Laura Bush had fun traveling around Texas. It gave her lots of time to admire the Texas scenery and have long conversations with her new husband. George's gift for relating to people impressed her. "He was just great, he was so terrific," she said. "He always said the right thing."[16]

A few months after their wedding, George Bush was scheduled to give a campaign speech in Muleshoe, Texas. He was delayed and could not get there in time to make the speech. He asked Laura to speak in his place.

Laura Bush nervously stood on the courthouse steps in Muleshoe. "My husband told me I'd never

Bush hoped to be elected to Congress.

have to make a political speech," she began. "So much for political promises."[17] After that, the speech dwindled down to nothing. Laura Bush spoke for a minute and a half and then sat down.

George W. Bush won the Republican primary in June 1978. He then faced Democratic candidate Kent Hance, a Texas state senator. Hance used campaign ads and speeches to portray Bush as a Yankee outsider and a spoiled rich kid. Laura Bush did not like it when an opponent or the press said negative things about her husband. Fiercely loyal, she supported him one hundred percent. "It's difficult," she said, "to hear things said about your husband."[18]

Mother-in-law Barbara Bush gave Laura some advice on being married to a politician. She told her not to criticize her husband's speeches. One night driving home from Lubbock to Midland, George Bush pestered Laura all the way home for her reaction to his speech. Laura avoided the question. Finally, as George Bush drove into the garage, he tried one last time to get Laura's reaction. "Tell me the truth," he asked. "How was my speech?"

For newlywed Laura, campaigning with George W. turned out to be fun.

"Well, it really wasn't great," said Laura.[19] Shocked at her answer, George Bush accidently drove into the garage wall.

George W. Bush lost the congressional election in November 1978. "Frankly, getting whipped was probably a pretty good thing for me," he said.[20] Many of his friends and supporters agreed. "That experience changed him, made him more humble," said local Republican Johnnye Davis.[21] With the election behind them, Laura Bush could focus her attention on turning her husband's messy house into a home—and, she hoped, starting a family.

5
BABIES AND
BASEBALL

Laura Bush settled into a comfortable routine as a homemaker after her husband lost the congressional election in 1978. While George Bush worked to build his oil company, she decorated their house, cooked her husband's favorite meals, gardened, and read. She organized her large collection of books the way books are arranged in a library. She arranged fiction titles alphabetically by the author's last name and biographies by the subject's last name. She volunteered with Midland's Junior League, a women's group that did charity work and held social functions.

On weekends, George and Laura Bush had fun with her parents or old friends. On Friday nights they ate Mexican food at their favorite restaurant. They often played cards around the kitchen table with Harold and

Jenna Welch. Sunday mornings found them in church and then out to lunch. Each summer, George and Laura joined the entire Bush clan in Kennebunkport, Maine, for a family vacation.

Laura and George Bush were eager to have children. "When George and I married, we wanted to have a lot of children—and then we didn't," she said.[1] In 1980, they decided to adopt. They visited the Gladney adoption home in Fort Worth, Texas, and filled out the necessary paperwork. They waited for a Gladney representative to visit their home and grant final approval for the adoption.

In January 1981, the Bushes flew to Washington, D.C., to watch George's father, George H.W. Bush, sworn in as vice president of the United States. They attended many of the inaugural festivities and socialized with well-known Republicans.

Two months later, in March 1981, Laura Bush was thrilled to learn she was pregnant. Her first sonogram revealed that she carried twins. Her husband sent her two dozen red roses "from the father of twins."[2] Laura's pregnancy was considered high risk. Her doctor told her to rest and take it easy. Because of her mother's history of miscarriages, Laura did not want to get her hopes up until the pregnancy was further along. She avoided the diaper aisle in the grocery store. She did not shop for baby clothes or furnish the nursery.

In the summer of 1981, Laura Bush stayed home

while her husband traveled to Kennebunkport for the Bush family vacation. But George was so worried about Laura, he flew back to Midland after one day in Maine. In September, Laura's doctor urged her to remain in bed for the rest of her pregnancy. He worried that the babies would be born too soon. Laura followed his advice. In October, she developed toxemia, a dangerous complication of pregnancy that threatened her life and the babies' lives. She was rushed to Baylor Hospital in Dallas.

The hospital staff monitored Laura Bush closely. The babies were not due for another seven weeks, around Christmastime. Her condition grew more serious. But she kept a positive attitude. "These babies are going to be born healthy," she told George.[3]

George Bush took a room in a hotel across the street from the hospital. He flew back and forth to Midland for work. Laura's determination calmed her frantic husband. "She was heroic," recalled George W. Bush. "There was an unbelievable will to protect the children. I remember to this day how confident I became because of her. She's a determined woman."[4]

By late November, Laura Bush was very ill. Her blood pressure had climbed to a dangerous level. The doctors called George at work in Midland and told him to come to Dallas. The babies would be delivered the next day. George Bush was stunned. "Are you sure?

It's five weeks early," he said. "Well, unless you want your wife's kidneys to fail," replied the doctor.[5]

On November 25, 1981, Laura Bush delivered two healthy baby girls by cesarean section. Following family tradition, Laura and George Bush named their daughters after their grandmothers: Jenna after Laura's mother, Jenna Welch, and Barbara after George's mother, Barbara Bush.

The new parents took their daughters home to Midland. George hired a part-time nurse to help his wife for the first few months. Laura recovered quickly. "Babies don't come with sets of instructions," she said.

The proud dad holds his twin daughters.

Laura and little Barbara at a rally to support the Reagan/Bush presidential campaign.

"Before George and I were married, we had a couple of theories on raising kids. Now we've got a couple of kids and no theories."[6]

Laura Bush felt lucky to be able to stay home and care for her daughters. Her favorite time with the babies was snuggling together in the early morning. "When they were infants," she said, "we would put them in bed with us in the mornings and George and I would each hold one of them."[7]

Laura Bush also enjoyed curling up on the couch with Barbara on one side, Jenna on the other and a picture book on her lap. She spent hours reading to them, just as her mother had read to her. George took a more active approach to reading. When he read the Dr. Seuss book *Hop on Pop*, he would lie on the floor and let the girls hop on him. Laura Bush often worked in the garden after Barbara and Jenna went to bed. "One night I was in the garden, the babies were asleep, safe in their beds, and I remember thinking, 'This is the life.'"[8]

Although her life seemed ideal, Laura Bush wanted to change one aspect of her marriage. For years, she had been asking her husband to stop drinking alcohol. "On the occasions where I drank too much she reminded me I was drinking too much," said George Bush. "And I listened."[9] With Laura's help, George Bush finally quit drinking in 1986, shortly after his fortieth birthday.

Laura Bush celebrated her fortieth birthday by taking a six-day river rafting trip through the Grand Canyon with a group of women friends. The group went white-water rafting and hiked ten miles up from the canyon floor on a steep, narrow trail.

When the price of oil dropped in the mid-1980s, George Bush sold his oil company. In April 1987, he decided to work full time on his father's presidential campaign. The family moved into a townhouse that was not far from the vice-presidential residence in Washington, D.C.

George Bush worked with his father and learned about national political campaigns. Laura cared for her six-year-old daughters and spent time with her mother-in-law. "It was the first time I'd ever lived in

Weekends with Gampy and Ganny

During their stay in Washington, Laura Bush and her six-year-old daughters spent nearly every weekend with George H. W. and Barbara Bush at the vice-president's house. The twins ate hamburgers for lunch and learned how to toss horseshoes with "gampy." One weekend, while George W. and Laura Bush were out of town campaigning, the twins stayed in the vice-presidential residence with their grandparents. George H. W. Bush was preparing for his second televised debate with Michael Dukakis when little Barbara interrupted. She could not find her stuffed dog Spikey. George H. W. Bush searched for the toy for over an hour. He finally located Spikey and tucked him into bed with his granddaughter.

the same town that his parents lived in and it gave Barbara Bush and me a chance to really become friends for the first time," she said.[10] The two women shared a love of reading and often swapped books.

In November 1988, George H.W. Bush became the forty-first president of the United States. After the president's inaugural ceremony in January 1989, Laura and George Bush and their young daughters, Jenna and Barbara, moved to Dallas, Texas. They bought a ranch-style house in a well-to-do neighborhood not far from Southern Methodist University. Oak trees surrounded the large home. It had a swimming pool and, to Laura's delight, a library.

In April 1989, George W. Bush purchased part ownership of the Texas Rangers, a major-league baseball team. He became one of the team's two managing general partners. As the official spokesman for the team, he made speeches to promote the Rangers. He tried to get more people

The Bush family enjoys spending time together in Maine.

interested in the team so they would buy tickets to the games. He put together a successful plan to build a new state-of-the-art baseball stadium in nearby Arlington.

Laura Bush's days revolved around her daughters' schedules. Barbara and Jenna attended a public school in Dallas, then transferred to the private, exclusive all-girls Hockaday School. Laura Bush volunteered in the school library, joined the parents' association, and drove in the carpool. "I've always done what really traditional women do, and I've been very, very satisfied," she said.[11] While Barbara and Jenna were in school, Laura Bush took classes on William Faulkner, Greek tragedy, and other literary topics. She also helped organize fund-raising events for various charities.

The Bushes attended nearly sixty Rangers baseball games a year. They sat right behind the dugout and

Laura and George W. Bush, with Jenna, left, and Barbara.

often ate dinner at the park's private club. Laura's parents frequently joined them. "Baseball's so slow you can daydream," said Laura Bush. "It's a very relaxing evening."[12]

Laura Bush learned a lot about baseball during her years as a Texas Rangers fan. She also learned to chew bubble gum. One night, after Laura blew a huge bubble during a game, her mother leaned over and told her blowing bubbles did not look very dignified. "Mother," replied Laura, "bubble gum is a tradition!"[13]

Laura, George, and the girls often visited President and Mrs. George H.W. Bush at Camp David, which is a presidential retreat seventy miles from the White House in the Catoctin Mountains of Maryland. They were also frequent visitors at the White House. Laura

Bush became familiar with the White House. She watched how her mother-in-law used her position as first lady to promote literacy.

President George H.W. Bush ran for reelection in 1992. Laura Bush dreaded reading newspapers during the campaign because of the negative stories that often appeared about her father-in-law. "It really hurts to see someone you love attacked," she said. "It gets to you after a while."[14] In November, President George H.W. Bush lost his reelection campaign. Bill Clinton became the forty-second president.

In 1993 George Bush decided the time was right for him to run for governor of Texas. Laura was not all that keen on the idea. She wanted to make sure it was something George truly wanted and not something he felt compelled to do because his name was George Bush. She also worried about her twelve-year-old daughters. She did not want them to lose their privacy and their chance to grow up like typical teens.

George Bush thought long and hard and decided to run. The problem was, just about everybody, including the entire Bush clan, thought incumbent governor Ann Richards was unbeatable.

Working For a More Literate America

Barbara Bush launched the Barbara Bush Foundation for Family Literacy in March 1989. The foundation has funded nearly five hundred family literacy programs in forty-seven states and the District of Columbia. She also supported the literacy program Reading Is Fundamental (RIF). Founded in 1966, RIF delivers free books to children and families who need them most.

6

FIRST LADY OF TEXAS

Once George W. Bush made the decision to run for governor of Texas, Laura Bush pushed aside her concerns and supported her husband. He faced a tough opponent in Governor Ann Richards, and both candidates engaged in rough campaign tactics. Richards verbally attacked George Bush throughout the campaign, calling him "Shrub," "Junior," and "Some Jerk." Bush ran ads that claimed Ann Richards was too lax on crime and had lowered the standards of public schools in Texas. George Bush also told voters that he was more "Texan" than Ann Richards. Laura Bush helped her husband remain calm during the campaign. She offered advice and encouragement. "She is a very wise person," said George Bush of his wife, "and when she talks, I pay close attention to what she has to say."[1]

Laura Bush did not do much campaigning for her husband. She spoke a few times at Republican Women's Clubs, but preferred to stay out of the spotlight. When she did speak in public, Laura Bush kept to a carefully prepared written speech. "I can't ad lib," she said. "I have to have a real speech that I virtually read."[2]

George W. Bush won the election in November 1994. On January 17, 1995, Laura Bush stood on the steps of the State Capitol in Austin, Texas and held a 150-year-old Bible. Her husband placed his hand on the Bible, recited the oath of office, and became the forty-sixth governor of Texas. After the swearing-in ceremony, guests enjoyed a barbecue lunch on the Capitol grounds, a parade, and lots of parties. Laura Bush attended them all as the new first lady of Texas.

Laura Bush was confident that her newly elected husband would make a fine governor of Texas.

As part of the inaugural festivities, Laura Bush invited seven award-winning Texas authors to give readings from their books at the Capitol. She was nervous about speaking at the event. "I knew I was going to have to speak at the reading, and I thought that the writers may not have voted for George," she said. "So I had an anxiety dream."[3] She dreamed she was sinking in Styrofoam. In spite of her jitters, the event was a huge success.

George, Laura, Barbara, and Jenna Bush moved from Dallas to the governor's mansion in Austin. They brought their two cats, Willie and Cowboy, and their dog Spot. Before long, they added another cat to the family. One morning, George Bush found a tiny kitten in a tree in the backyard of the governor's mansion. The kitten had six toes on each paw. His paws looked like baseball gloves. The family named him Ernie after the famous author Ernest Hemingway, who had six-toed cats.

Laura Bush enrolled thirteen-year-old twins Jenna and Barbara at St. Andrew's Episcopal School. She asked the press to leave her daughters alone. She did not want photographers taking their pictures and would not allow reporters to interview them. "I think that our children ought to be totally left alone and allowed to have a totally private life," she said. "They're not public citizens. They didn't run for office."[4]

Her first priority was taking care of her family. She

worked to make the governor's mansion a home. She brought in her own furniture for the family portion of the house so George and the girls would feel comfortable. She added her own decorating touches to the historic home. In the public areas of the mansion, Laura Bush displayed paintings by Texas artists. She also hung vintage art in the State Capitol. She covered the walls of her office in the basement of the Capitol with paintings by Texas artists and rotated the paintings throughout the year to showcase different artists.

Laura Bush used a large black binder to keep track

Laura Bush's first priority was her family, but she had a hectic schedule as first lady of Texas.

of her hectic schedule as first lady of Texas. Her monthly schedule was on one side of a chart, with the governor's schedule on the other. She gave Barbara and Jenna a typed daily schedule of where she and their father would be each day. Laura Bush made sure she was home by 4 P.M. so she could greet her daughters when they came home from school.

On April 29, 1995, Laura Bush's eighty-two-year-old father, Harold Welch, died. He suffered from Alzheimer's disease. The family gathered in Midland for the funeral at the First United Methodist Church, the church where Laura and George had been married. Laura Bush was very close to her father and grieved deeply.

Over time, Laura Bush grew comfortable with her role as first lady of Texas. She realized she could use her position to improve things she cared about: reading and literacy. "Well, if I'm going to be a public figure, I might as well do what I've always liked doing," she said, "which meant acting like a librarian and getting people interested in reading."[5] Laura Bush traveled around Texas visiting schools and giving speeches. She talked about literacy and reading programs for children.

As first lady of Texas, she found that people listened to what she had to say. Although it was difficult for her, Laura Bush worked hard to improve her public-speaking skills. The first time George Bush heard her speak, he was amazed. "I feature myself as an OK speaker," he said. "I feature my mother as a fabulous speaker. And Laura was better than both of us."[6]

National Republican leaders noticed Laura Bush's growing popularity. In the summer of 1996 they invited her to deliver a prime-time speech at the Republican National Convention in San Diego, California. She spoke about the importance of teaching children to read. "Reading is to the mind what food is to the body," she said. "George and I will not be satisfied until every child in Texas, each and every child, learns to read."[7] After hearing Laura speak at the convention, George Bush said, "Right then I realized that the same thing was

Laura Bush used her status as a public figure to visit schools and encourage reading and literacy.

> **"Reading is to the mind what food is to the body."**

happening to me that had happened to my old man. I was already becoming less popular than my own wife."[8]

Laura Bush put her ideas for increasing literacy into action. In 1996, with money from the Barbara Bush Foundation, she created the First Lady's Family Literacy Initiative for Texas. This program gives grants to family literacy programs. Grant money is used to develop reading readiness programs for young children and to improve reading skills of entire families. Young children and adults are taught together. Parents learn to help their children improve their reading skills.

Another program Laura Bush brought to Texas was Reach Out and Read, which had been started in Boston for infants and toddlers. When a baby and mother see a doctor for a well-child visit, the doctor gives the child a book to take home and keep. The doctor also talks to the mother about the importance of reading to her child.

In the fall of 1996, Barbara and Jenna Bush transferred to Austin High School. They often invited their friends to the governor's mansion. Laura Bush enjoyed having a houseful of teens, but did not approve of her daughters' favorite television programs, *Beverly Hills 90210* and *Melrose Place*. She told Barbara and Jenna, "Those aren't my values," though she continued to let them watch the shows.[9]

In November 1996, Laura Bush organized the first Texas Book Festival, "a celebration of words, reading, and published works."[10] Booths and tents were set up around the state Capitol for the three-day festival. Texas authors read from their work. There were panel discussions, storytellers, and children's activities. Musical groups entertained and clowns performed while thousands of people strolled around the Capitol grounds.

The festival raised more than $260,000 from the sale of books, T-shirts, a silent auction, and a gala. The money raised was given to Texas libraries. Laura Bush also worked on increasing awareness of women's health issues like breast cancer and osteoporosis.

As first lady of Texas, Laura Bush hosted many social functions at the governor's mansion. She preferred barbecues to black-tie events. She held her high school reunion in a tent on the lawn of the mansion. It rained the night of the party, so the first lady of Texas kicked off her shoes, sloshed around with the other guests, and danced to golden oldies.

When the demands of public life started to crowd out her privacy, Laura Bush spent time with her girlfriends. They often took long walks around Austin's Town Lake and went on summer retreats, hiking or rafting in the West. She also enjoyed the outdoors and wide-open spaces of the Bushes' 1,600-acre ranch in Crawford, Texas.

Laura Bush was an extremely popular governor's

wife. After meeting her, a wealthy El Paso man named his racehorse Sweet Laura Bush. A businessman plastered her name on the gas tank of his Harley-Davidson motorcycle. But in spite of her popularity, Laura Bush did not seek the limelight. As first lady, she was required to travel about with a Department of Public Safety trooper for protection. Once, she stood in line with her trooper to buy a cup of coffee in the basement cafeteria of the Capitol. The man in front of her saw the trooper and asked her, "I wonder who's in here?" Laura Bush looked around and said, "I don't know."[11]

In the fall of 1998, George Bush sold the Texas Rangers baseball team for a huge profit. He also ran for reelection as governor of Texas. Laura Bush took a much more active role in this campaign than she had in the past. She had gained confidence as a speaker and could even poke fun at her husband in her speeches. She often told her audience, "George thinks a bibliography is the story of the guys who wrote the Bible."[12] After her audience stopped laughing, she would smile and let them know she was kidding.

George Bush appreciated Laura's contributions to his first term as governor. "There are many reasons I want people to reelect me as Governor of Texas," he said. "The most important one may be to keep Laura Bush as our First Lady."[13] Bush won the election on November 4, 1998, with nearly 70 percent of the vote.

Laura Bush continued her efforts to improve

literacy in Texas. She worked with the state legislature to help write Senate Bill 955 to improve early childhood education. The bill, known among Texas lawmakers as Laura Bush's Bill, set aside more than $215 million for reading programs for children and adults. One of the programs, Ready to Read, helps thousands of low-income children in preschool with

After being sworn in for his second term as governor, the Bushes rode in the inaugural parade in Austin, Texas.

beginning reading skills such as learning letters and letter sounds.

In the spring of 1999, George Bush honored his wife for all the work she had done for literacy. He had a tree-lined brick walkway, just outside the library at Southern Methodist University, built in her name. "This is a gift that reflects its namesake," said George Bush at the dedication of the Laura Bush Promenade. "This is a serene and peaceful place, just like Laura."[14] Choked with emotion, his eyes glistening with tears, George Bush could not finish his speech. Laura hugged her husband and quietly led him to his seat.

George Bush's popularity in Texas caused Republican leaders to encourage him to run for president in 2000. His father, George H.W. Bush, had been the forty-first president, so George and Laura knew the challenges that came with the job. The country had seen only one father-son combination of presidents— John Adams, who served as the nation's second president from 1797 to 1801, and John Quincy Adams, who served as the sixth president from 1825 to 1829.

Laura and George Bush discussed the question for months. It was not an easy decision. "I'm reluctant," said Laura. "Absolutely. It's a major life change. I'm not particularly worried about safety. Privacy. I'm very worried about privacy."[15]

7

ELECTION 2000

Laura Bush accomplished a great deal as first lady of Texas, and she enjoyed her job. She liked living in Austin and had a large circle of friends. Her husband and daughters were healthy and happy and she lived close enough to her mother for frequent visits. "I had the perfect life for myself in Austin," she said.[1]

She worried about losing too much privacy if her husband ran for president. In Austin, she could slip out of the governor's mansion to take a walk or meet her friends for lunch. If George W. Bush ran for president, she would become a national figure. Secret Service agents would follow her every move. She did not want the details of her family's private life plastered across newspapers and television sets.

The Bushes knew their lives would change dramatically if George W. ran for president.

Laura Bush also worried about the effect the campaign would have on her daughters. Barbara and Jenna did not want their father to run for president. They were finishing their senior year of high school and getting ready to start college. Barbara and Jenna did not want to live in the national spotlight, with reporters and photographers hounding them. They wanted to start college like thousands of other freshmen around the country. Laura Bush shared her daughters' concerns.

Laura Bush dreaded the negative publicity a national campaign would bring. She reminded her husband of the bitter battle his father, George H.W. Bush, had fought in the 1992 campaign. "I know what the ugly side of politics is," she said. "The '92 race was miserable. It's very difficult to have bad things said about the people you love."[2]

Laura Bush asked her husband to think about why he wanted to be president. She told him to examine his motives and make sure he was running for the right reasons. George Bush convinced Laura that he wanted to run for president because he thought he would be a good leader for the United States. She agreed. Once he made the decision, Laura supported her husband completely. According to her mother-in-law, Barbara Bush, Laura's philosophy was, "You can either like it or not, so you might as well like it."[3]

Laura and George Bush campaigned together. "I

know him best and I have the opportunity to tell people a viewpoint of him that they might not have or might not know," she said.[4] George Bush often sought Laura's advice. She did not try to influence public policy, but she did offer her opinions to her husband. "I trust her judgment a lot," said George Bush.[5]

During the campaign, Laura Bush became an invaluable sounding board for her husband. Once, while his parents were visiting the ranch in Crawford, Texas, George Bush could not decide on the correct wording for an upcoming speech. Instead of asking his father's advice, Bush told his staff, "Read it to Laura. See what she thinks."[6]

Laura did not try to influence public policy, but she did offer her opinions to her husband.

Although Laura Bush campaigned for her husband, she protected her daughters from publicity. They did not campaign for their father. When a *Newsweek* reporter found out Barbara's SAT score, Laura Bush called the magazine and asked them not to publish the score. "Barbara would be so embarrassed," she said.[7]

During the summer of 2000, in addition to campaigning for her husband, Laura helped their daughters get ready for college. In the fall, Barbara would start classes at Yale University, the school her father and grandfather had attended. Jenna would attend the

University of Texas at Austin, where her mother had attended graduate school.

Laura Bush also supervised construction of a new ranch house in Crawford, Texas. The property, twenty-five miles west of Waco, had steep canyons, a bass-filled fishing pond, and a large grove of oak trees. She worked closely with an architect to design the house to fit into the landscape. The low, narrow house was built of limestone native to the area. Most of the rooms have floor-to-ceiling windows. George Bush appreciated Laura's ability to juggle so many tasks. "Laura is able to live an interesting life that is apart from the political campaign, which I find totally appealing," he said. "Politics doesn't totally consume her, and as a result, it doesn't totally consume me."[8]

On July 31, 2000, the Republican Party met in Philadelphia to formally nominate George W. Bush as their presidential candidate. Laura Bush gave the first major speech of the convention. It was the biggest speech of her life. Her voice and image were shown to millions of television viewers. When she walked on stage in a lime-green suit, the audience applauded. And applauded. Laura held up her hands and said, "Okay, that's enough," just as she used to calm her second-grade students.[9]

Laura Bush's warmth and sincerity charmed the convention. "I am honored—and a little over-whelmed—to help open the convention that will nominate my husband for President of the United States," she said. "You know I am completely objective when I say—you have made a GREAT choice."[10]

Her speech focused on education and how her husband had been able to work with both Democrats and Republicans to solve problems as governor of Texas. She talked about growing up in Midland, her career as a teacher, and her family. "They say parents often have to get out of the house when their kids go off to college because it seems so lonely," she said. "Everyone deals with it in different ways. But I told George I thought running for President was a little extreme."[11] While she was speaking, the crowd interrupted her thirty times with applause.

After the convention, Laura Bush campaigned on her own in twenty-four states. The press often asked what role she saw for herself in the White House. "I've traveled all over our state working on issues dealing with education, libraries and breast cancer awareness. So, if I were to become the First Lady, I'd be working on those same issues," she said.[12] Voters liked what they saw in Laura Bush. Her husband's popularity grew.

The closer it got to election day, the harder Laura Bush campaigned. She joined her mother-in-law, Barbara Bush, and future Secretary of State Condoleezza Rice on a bus tour. They worked to get women to vote for George Bush. They told voters the "W" in George W. Bush's name stood for "women."

During the campaign, one of George W. Bush's supporters handed Laura this sign.

As Laura Bush's prominence in the campaign grew, so did the attention of the media. The press analyzed her every word and questioned her when her remarks seemed to differ from her husband's. "If I differ with my husband, I'm not going to tell you about it," Laura Bush told one reporter.[13]

By September 2000, the candidates were neck and neck in the polls. Political experts predicted one of the closest elections in history. The strain was starting to show on high-strung George Bush. His media adviser, Mark McKinnon, suggested Laura Bush travel with her husband.

Laura Bush joined George on the campaign trail. His staff immediately noticed a change in their boss. "She brought calm and serenity to his bearing," said Mark McKinnon. "He was happier, more at ease, less distracted. Even on the airplane, he was more likely to relax. If she wasn't there, he'd bounce around the plane."[14] One of the ways Laura helped her husband relieve stress was through gentle teasing. "We do tease each other," she said. "We've had a million nicknames for each other—ridiculous names."[15] Their latest nickname for each other is "Bushie."[16]

On election day, November 7, 2000, the results flip-flopped between the two candidates. At first it looked as if Vice President Al Gore, the Democratic candidate for president, had won the election. The press reported that the majority of voters in Florida, a key state, had voted for Gore. Then, George Bush seemed to move ahead when later results in Florida were announced. Finally, George W. Bush was declared the winner in the early hours of the morning. Vice President Gore called Bush to concede the election.

Two hours later, Gore took back his concession when it turned out that the state of Florida was "too close to call." Officials in Florida would have to recount the votes.

Plenty Tough

Although Laura Bush tries to keep her advice to her husband private, she does not hesitate to offer her opinion if she feels George Bush needs it. "Laura can be plenty tough, and she can chew him out," said Robert McCleskey. "I saw them once, when he was giving orders to all these people and rattling off commands, and she just looked at him and said, 'Bushie, you're not president yet!'"[17] George Bush appreciates his wife's candor. "She's pretty good at keeping me centered and reminding me that I'm not 'it,'" he said.[18]

Days passed. Laura Bush waited with the rest of the nation to see who would be the next president. On November 10, 2000, in spite of the chaos surrounding the election results, Laura Bush spoke at the fifth annual Texas Book Festival at the State Capitol in Austin. The crowd gave her a standing ovation. "This is an event where the outcome is never in doubt," she said.[19]

Campaign workers noticed that Laura Bush's presence had a calming effect on her husband.

Protestors upset about the election milled around in front of the Texas Capitol. They chanted and carried signs. Some supported Bush, others Gore. But the demonstration was peaceful and did not dampen the spirits of the festival authors and guests. One hundred forty authors from around the country took part in the book festival, which had become one of the most important literary events in the Southwest. The 2000 festival put the total earnings for Texas libraries from Texas Book Festivals at more than one million dollars.

After the festival, Laura and George Bush went to their ranch in Crawford, Texas, to wait for the election results to be finalized. While officials in Florida began to recount the votes, lawyers haggled over the election results for weeks. The issue was finally brought before the U.S. Supreme Court to decide whether all the votes in Florida would be recounted or not. Laura Bush surprised many people during this waiting period with her calm and steady manner. "Both of us have a belief that everything is going to be alright, whatever the outcome is," she said. "We are happily married and are going to be happily married when this is over."[20]

On December 12, 2000, the Supreme Court decided to stop the recount of votes in Florida. Florida Secretary of State Katherine Harris certified George W. Bush as the winner in Florida. With Florida's twenty-five electoral votes, Bush would become the forty-third president of the United States. Laura Bush had lunch with her Austin garden club the next afternoon. "Laura, it's all over!" said one of her friends. "No," said Laura. "It's just beginning."[21]

8
AMERICA'S
FIRST LADY

With the election behind them, Laura Bush and her family looked forward to some quiet family time over the holidays. They knew the presidential inauguration would keep them busy in January. On Christmas Day, 2000, the family had lunch with friends in Austin. Nineteen-year-old Jenna left the table with a stomachache. The family went home to the governor's mansion. All afternoon, Jenna's pain got worse. At 5 P.M., Laura Bush rushed her daughter to St. David's Hospital.

At the hospital, doctors told Laura Bush that Jenna needed an emergency operation to remove her appendix. The operation went well. Laura Bush stayed with her daughter in the hospital. She slept on a fold-out sleeper sofa beside Jenna's bed. Laura Bush spent the rest of

December taking care of Jenna. She also began to prepare for her husband's inauguration as president of the United States.

As part of inauguration week, one event honors the new first lady. Laura Bush changed the focus of the event. "I'd like to depart from that tradition," said Laura Bush, "by making this occasion a tribute to the thousands of people who have affected my life and all of our lives—our great American authors."[1] She would devote the evening to readings by five American writers. Laura Bush joked that the event was a librarian's dream. "Not only do we get to hear from five respected American authors but also, if anybody in the audience starts to get rowdy, I get to tell them to hush up," she said.[2] George Bush spoke briefly at the event. He said of Laura, "Her love for books is real. Her love for children is real. My love for her is real."[3] The audience jumped to their feet and clapped wildly.

On January 20, 2001, Laura Bush stood beside her husband on the Capitol steps in Washington, D.C. George W. Bush took the oath of office and became the forty-third president of the United States. Laura Bush's second-grade teacher, Charlene Gnagy, watched from a place of honor.

After the inauguration, Laura and George Bush walked down Pennsylvania Avenue as part of the inaugural parade. They held hands and smiled in the freezing rain. The Bushes went to eight inaugural balls

The first lady celebrated her husband's election at a number of inaugural balls.

Laura Bush's Fashion Savvy

Laura Bush had to make several adjustments to life in the national spotlight. One area that changed a great deal was her fashion savvy. "I've never been that interested in clothes," she said. "Before I had the job as first lady of Texas, I wore jeans, pants, and T-shirts."[4] She liked clothes in camel and gray. As her husband's political ambitions pushed her into the public eye, Laura Bush bought a whole new wardrobe, with brightly colored suits that show up well on television. She now works with famous fashion designers.

First Lady Laura Bush was surprised at the amount of attention paid to her hair and clothes. She wanted people to listen to what she had to say, not focus on how she looked. "I don't know that I'm trying to say anything with my appearance," she said. "I hope I'm saying something with my actions."[5]

that night. Laura Bush wore a red dress of beaded Chantilly lace. The dress had thousands of Austrian crystal beads. Diamonds and rubies sparkled in her necklace and earrings.

The Bushes moved from the governor's mansion in Austin, Texas, to the White House in Washington, D.C. "One advantage here is that all the rooms are already beautifully furnished," said Laura Bush. "I didn't feel obligated to bring anything."[6] She brought family photos, clothes, and their pets, Spot, an eleven-year-old dog, and Barney, a Scottish terrier puppy. They brought their cat, India, but left their six-toed cat Ernie with a friend in California. With his claws, Laura Bush feared he might rip up the antique furniture and curtains in the White House.

Laura Bush had visited the White House many times when her father-in-law, George H.W. Bush, had been vice president and president. "We already knew the White House," she said. "We knew our way around . . . and not only that, we knew all the staff."[7] She enjoyed rearranging the furniture in her new home. Bush took out several pieces and replaced them with antiques she found in storage. She brought back Jacqueline Kennedy's favorite velvet chairs. She also decorated the rooms Barbara and Jenna would use when they visited from college.

The first lady's office was traditionally housed in the East Wing of the White House. When Hillary Rodham Clinton became first lady in 1993, she moved her office to the West Wing. The West Wing contains the executive offices of the president. Hillary Clinton wanted to be close to the president so she could be involved with policy-making decisions. Laura Bush moved her office back to the East Wing. Although she would be an active first lady, she did not plan to take part in the policy-making of the new administration. She hung paintings from the White House collection on the walls of her office and filled the bookshelves with children's books. Laura Bush did not like the title "First Lady." She told her staff of seventeen to answer the phone "Mrs. Bush's Office" and sign her letters "Laura Bush."

Two weeks after the inauguration, Laura Bush left Washington and flew to Crawford, Texas. She finished decorating their new ranch house. She picked out

The Bushes gave a press conference outside their ranch home in Crawford, Texas.

furniture and had native grasses, bluebonnets, and honeysuckle planted around the house. She also directed the planting of an alley of oak trees to line the long driveway. Laura Bush knew that their time in Washington was temporary. They would have the ranch for the rest of their lives. She wanted to make it a special place for her family. "It's a haven for us," she said, where we "want to grow old."[8]

When Laura Bush returned to Washington, the press asked her over and over again what kind of first lady she would be. "I think I'll just be Laura Bush," she said.[9] "I have a lifelong passion for introducing children to the magic of words. I am proud of my efforts on behalf of the children of Texas and I look forward to building those efforts on behalf of all American schoolchildren."[10]

Laura Bush threw herself into her work. In February 2001, she launched her Ready to Read, Ready to Learn education program. The program had two goals. The first goal was to make sure that when children start school, they are ready to learn to read. Bush wanted to increase preschool programs that build prereading and vocabulary skills. She also wanted to add a reading program to the preschool program Head Start.

The second part of Ready to Read, Ready to Learn was aimed at making sure each child had a well-trained teacher. Laura Bush supported several programs designed to recruit more teachers. Teach for America encouraged recent college graduates to teach for two years in disadvantaged schools. Troops to Teachers urged men and women retiring from the military to enter classrooms as teachers.

In May 2001, *People* magazine named Laura Bush one of the fifty most beautiful people in the world. Her picture appeared in the magazine along with forty-nine other celebrities, including Tom Cruise, Julia Roberts, and Michael Jordan. In the article, Laura Bush shared her secret to looking and feeling great. "I drink water all day," she said.[11] President Bush was pleased. "I am glad that Americans are getting a chance to find out something I've known for 23 years," he said. "Laura Bush is a beautiful person, inside and out."[12]

The most difficult problem Laura Bush faced in the early months of her husband's presidency was dealing with the national spotlight on her daughters. The nineteen-year-old Bush twins, Jenna and Barbara, were issued tickets for alcohol possession by a minor. Jenna was also charged with using someone else's driver's license to purchase alcohol. The girls were required to perform community service, attend alcohol awareness classes, and pay fines.

George and Laura Bush had asked the press not to write about their daughters. They wanted them to be able to lead private lives, like other college freshman.

However, when the girls were involved in one alcohol-related incident after another, the press had a field day. Headlines around the world screamed, "Oops! They Did It Again," and "Double Trouble."

Laura Bush worried about a heredity predisposition to alcoholism because of her husband's struggle with alcohol. She also felt that the press were too focused on Barbara and Jenna, whose behavior, unfortunately, was typical of many college students. Above all, she felt the issue was a private family problem and should not be discussed in the national media.

"Gee, Bushie"

When her picture appeared as one of *People* magazine's fifty most-beautiful people, Laura Bush could not resist teasing her husband. "Gee, Bushie," she said when she saw the magazine, "I don't see your face in here . . ."[13]

Keeping daughters Barbara, left, and Jenna, out of the spotlight was a challenge.

The family met at Camp David. Laura and George Bush discussed the seriousness of alcohol abuse with their daughters. They reminded Jenna of the Texas three-strikes rule, which George Bush had signed into law when he was governor. If Jenna committed one more alcohol-related offense, she faced mandatory jail time. Jenna and Barbara promised their parents that they would stay away from alcohol until they turned twenty-one.

With her daughters back in school, Laura Bush joined her husband in June 2001 on his first official visit to Europe. She visited museums, schools, libraries, and gardens. At the Leaning Tower of Pisa in Pisa, Italy, crowds appeared and called her name. "It was rather shocking," she said. "There were huge crowds lined up, and their response was just funny—calling 'Mrs. Bush! Mrs. Bush!' and clapping."[14]

In July 2001, Laura Bush hosted a childhood education summit with U.S. Secretary of Education Rod Paige and U.S. Secretary of Health and Human Services Tommy G. Thompson. Experts described what parents and teachers can do to prepare babies and young children for reading and learning. Laura Bush spoke at the event. She shared her experience as a teacher and how she could have used expert advice on the best way to teach reading. "I had instruction in

Laura Bush at the Leaning Tower of Pisa in Italy. With her is Francesco Pacini, who runs the organization that oversees Pisa's historical monuments.

teaching reading, of course, but in practice, I didn't know how to teach a child to read. I had to learn my own techniques as my students learned."[15] At the conference, child development experts from around the country shared the latest research about brain development in young children and how that affects learning.

On July 30, 2001, Laura Bush announced plans for the first-ever National Book Festival, to be held on September 8. "I look forward to welcoming book lovers of all ages to our nation's capital to celebrate the magic of reading and storytelling," she said.[16] She also announced the creation of the Laura Bush Foundation for America's Libraries. It would give grants to school libraries across the country to purchase books. "My lifelong passion for books and reading began when I was a little girl," said Laura Bush. "This new Foundation provides yet another opportunity to share with America's children the magical world of books and reading."[17]

In addition to her hectic schedule promoting literacy programs and traveling with the president, Laura Bush hosted formal parties at the White House. Her first state dinner, on Wednesday, September 5, 2001, welcomed Mexican President Vicente Fox and his wife, Martha. The guest list of one hundred thirty included actor Clint Eastwood and opera singer Placido Domingo. After an elegant dinner and dancing, guests enjoyed a twenty-minute fireworks display to end the evening.

The next day, Laura Bush hosted a tea in the Green Room of the White House for Mexico's first lady, Martha Sahagun de Fox. The two first ladies also visited an exhibit of Latino art at the Terra Museum of American Art in Chicago, Illinois.

Over the weekend, Laura Bush hosted the first National Book Festival. Some of her friends from Texas who had worked with her on the Texas Book Festival stayed at the White House as her guests. Laura Bush and her friends enjoyed visiting with each other. They also enjoyed the book festival, so much like the one they had helped to organize for Texas.

Of all her many jobs, Laura Bush considered taking care of her husband her top priority. She was the center of his emotional support. George Bush often read his speeches to her and asked for feedback. She read four newspapers a day and knew what the press wrote about her husband. "She's got a great sense of how the President is perceived. She looks out for that," said media expert Mark McKinnon. "She has a good sense of when his message is not being communicated well and received the way it should be."[18]

George W. Bush would need every bit of his wife's support in the days and weeks ahead.

9

COMFORTER-IN-CHIEF

On Tuesday, September 11, 2001, Laura Bush woke to a sunny, clear day in Washington, D.C. She was scheduled to testify before the Senate Education Committee on early childhood education. She stepped out of the White House shortly before 9 A.M. When she reached her car, one of her Secret Service officers leaned over and whispered into her ear. An airplane had crashed into the north tower of the World Trade Center in New York City. Laura Bush and her staff thought it must have been an accident. They drove, as scheduled, to Capitol Hill.

On the short ride to the Capitol, Laura Bush learned that a second plane had crashed into the south tower of the Trade Center. Now there could be no doubt. America was under attack. Senator Edward Kennedy, head of the education committee, met Laura Bush at the door of the Senate office building. He told her he was going to postpone the education hearing and then led her to his office.

Senator Kennedy and Laura Bush waited together for news. "I felt as if we were going through the motions, pretending to be normal, when we all knew 'normal' would never again be what we knew it to be on September 10th," she said.[1] Kennedy had brought his dog, Splash, to work with him that day. While they waited, Splash rested his head on Laura Bush's knee. "There was something very comforting about that," she said.[2]

> "We all knew 'normal' would never again be what we knew it to be on September 10th."

At 9:30 Laura Bush spoke to the reporters who were at the Capitol to cover the hearing. "Our hearts and prayers go out to the victims of terrorism," she said, "and our support goes to the rescue workers."[3] She fought back tears as she talked about the children of America. "We need to reassure them that many people love them and care for them, and that while there are some bad people in the world, there are many more good people."[4]

At 9:43 a third plane hit the Pentagon in Washington, D.C. Government officials feared that the White House and Capitol buildings might be in danger of attack. Secret Service agents rushed Laura Bush to a safe location. Police closed off the Capitol and the White House and marked the area with yellow plastic crime scene tape.

President Bush was in Florida visiting an elementary school when he heard about the attacks. He called his wife. When Laura Bush finished talking to her husband, she called her daughters at college. Then she called her mother. "I called my mother, and she thinks I called to reassure her that I was OK, but the fact is, I called to hear her voice and to have her reassure me."[5]

Laura Bush spent the rest of the day watching the news unfold on television. She watched the one-hundred-ten-story south tower of the World Trade Center collapse. She learned that another plane had crashed in Shanksville, Pennsylvania. Then she watched the north tower collapse. Thousands were feared dead in the worst terrorist attack in American history.

Vice President Dick Cheney urged President Bush not to return to Washington right away. Cheney and the Secret Service did not think it was safe. George Bush flew to an air force base in Louisiana, then to another in Nebraska. At 4:30 P.M. he called Laura and told her he was going back to Washington. "See you at the White House," he said. "Love you, go on home."[6]

President Bush called the attacks "acts of war."[7] He promised to use "all necessary and appropriate force" to punish those responsible.[8] He called up reserve units of

President Bush showed his support in New York City after the attack on the World Trade Center.

the Armed Forces and the Coast Guard to active duty. His advisers identified Osama bin Laden, the leader of a terrorist group in Afghanistan, as a prime suspect in the attacks. Bush vowed to capture bin Laden "dead or alive."[9] Laura Bush was not happy with her husband's strong words. "Tone it down, darling," she told him.[10]

While the president met with his security advisers, talked to leaders around the world, and put together a plan, Laura Bush comforted the nation. She started with her staff at the White House. "She met with all of us to make sure we were OK," said Ashleigh Adams, an aide to Laura Bush. "She provided some words of comfort and inspiration, about how this was an opportunity for all of us to showcase what the American spirit is all about, about being resilient and caring for one another."[11]

Laura Bush visited wounded survivors of the Pentagon attack at Walter Reed Army Medical Center. She wrote letters to reassure America's children. One letter went to elementary school children, the other to middle and high school students. The letters were sent to school superintendents across the country.

President Bush named Friday, September 14, 2001, a day of national prayer and remembrance. Laura Bush organized a memorial service at the Washington National Cathedral. The service was broadcast on television. There were prayers from religious leaders of many faiths and a sermon by Reverend

Elementary School Letter

September 12, 2001

Dear Children:

Many Americans were injured or lost their lives in the recent national tragedy. All their friends and loved ones are feeling very sad, and you may be feeling sad, frightened, or confused, too.

I want to reassure you that many people—including your family, your teachers, and your school counselor—love and care about you and are looking out for your safety. You can talk with them and ask them questions. You can also write down your thoughts or draw a picture that shows how you are feeling and share that with the adults in your life.

When sad or frightening things happen, all of us have an opportunity to become better people by thinking about others. We can show them we care about them by saying so and by doing nice things for them. Helping others will make you feel better, too.

I want you to know how much I care about all of you. Be kind to each other, take care of each other, and show your love for each other.

With best wishes,
Laura Bush[12]

Billy Graham. Laura Bush chose the hymns for the service. The beautiful music of the Cathedral choirs and the United States Navy Sea Chanters soothed the thousands of mourners packed into the cathedral.

On September 17, Laura Bush traveled to Shanksville, Pennsylvania, and spoke at the memorial service for United Flight 93, which had crashed in the countryside. "I want each of you to know today that you are not alone," she said. "We cannot ease the pain, but this country stands by you."[13] Then she met with the victims' families and offered quiet words of encouragement to each one. "She thinks about other people all the time," said Reverend Kathleene Card, associate pastor of Trinity United Methodist Church and the wife of White House Chief of Staff Andrew Card. "She is constantly watching to see if other people are being taken care of. That is a part of her. That is who she is."[14]

The next day, September 18, Laura Bush traveled to Chicago to appear on *The Oprah Winfrey Show.* The television show gave Laura Bush a chance to speak to parents and teachers about how to help their children deal with the September 11 tragedy. "I want every parent

As a guest on *The Oprah Winfrey Show,* Laura Bush talked about helping children cope with their fears after the attack.

to put their arms around their children and reassure them that they're loved and cared for," she said.[15]

Laura Bush appeared on dozens of television shows. On each one, she repeated her message: comfort and protect the children. She asked parents to turn off their television sets, talk with their children, listen to them, and tell them they are safe and loved. She asked families to share meals together and read stories before bed.

Like any mother, Laura Bush wanted to see her daughters. The Secret Service told her it would be easier to keep them safe if they stayed on their college campuses. Laura agreed, but it was difficult for her not to be able to hug her girls. Instead, she called them every day. When asked what she said to them, she replied, "We tell them we love them. . . . And if they're not there, we leave a message. 'This is our call to tell you number one, we love you, and number two, we love you.'"[16]

On September 20, President George Bush spoke to the nation from the Capitol. He had learned that Al Qaeda, a terrorist group based in the Middle East, had carried out the September 11 attack. The leader of this group, Osama bin Laden, was believed to be hiding in Afghanistan. On October 7, the president ordered military troops into Afghanistan.

With American soldiers fighting abroad, George Bush needed his wife's support more than ever. He often reached for her hand in public, and she did all she could to make his life less stressful. When she was traveling, she called one of George's fraternity brothers and asked him to visit the president while she was away. "Since September 11 I've had the opportunity, or maybe I should say, the responsibility, to be steady for our country, and for my husband," she said.[17]

Laura Bush was calm and reassuring to her husband and the public. She faced her private fears alone. She often woke up in the middle of the night, worried about another terrorist attack. "I was nervous, I was anxious," she said.[18] To relieve her own stress, Laura Bush found relief in the calming influence of books. "I read a lot," she said, "and a lot of times I can lose myself in the book even when I'm anxious. Reading is certainly a way that I've handled stress—as well as loneliness, as well as boredom, as well as any other thing during my life that I've had to deal with."[19]

> **Laura Bush was calm and reassuring to her husband and the public.**

Laura Bush visited several elementary schools around the country and read to students. She chose books that encouraged children to show kindness to people of different cultures and religions. She also visited the New York fire station of Battalion 9, which lost half its men on September 11. She left a bouquet of sunflowers tied with a red, white, and blue ribbon. "You showed the world that honor and bravery are alive in

New York City," she wrote in a journal at the station. "Thank you for being heroes. God bless you."[20]

On November 8, Laura Bush spoke at the National Press Club in Washington, D.C. She shared some of her experiences traveling the country. "I've seen people helping strangers; I've seen strangers becoming heroes; I've seen this country at its best. Americans are proud and we care about others."[21]

The press praised Laura Bush's actions after September 11. They began calling her Comforter-in-Chief and First Mom. Bush's longtime friend Nancy Weiss expressed the thoughts of many when she said, "I feel that she has her arms around the country."[22]

On November 17, 2001, Laura Bush gave the president's weekly radio address. It was the first time in history a first lady gave an entire presidential radio address. She talked about how poorly women were treated in Afghanistan. "The plight of women and children in Afghanistan is a matter of deliberate human cruelty," she said. "I hope Americans will join our family in working to insure that dignity and opportunity will be secured for all the women and children of Afghanistan."[23]

Due to increased security at the White House, public tours had been canceled. Laura Bush invited a television crew to film the White House holiday decorations so the country would be able to enjoy them. The theme she had chosen was Home for the Holidays.

Never before in history had a first lady given the president's weekly radio address. Laura Bush talked about the oppression of women in Afghanistan.

Forty-nine artificial snow-covered fir trees spread across the main floor. They were trimmed with ornaments modeled after each former president's home. In the State Dining Room sat a 130-pound gingerbread house designed to look like the White House of 1800.

As the year 2001 came to a close, Laura Bush encouraged Americans to get back to their normal routines. "An act of terror is meant to undermine a country, make us feel vulnerable, make us be afraid," she said on the television show *Larry King Live.* "And what happened instead, I think, is it made us realize how strong we are and how unified we are as a country."[24] Laura Bush, as America's Comforter-in-Chief, helped bring about that unity and heal the wounds of a grieving nation.

10
ON THE
WORLD STAGE

As a teacher, librarian, and governor's wife, Laura Bush promoted reading and literacy for America's children. As first lady, she expanded her vision to include the children of the world. On January 24, 2002, she became the fourth first lady to testify before Congress. She spoke before the Senate Education Committee and gave the speech she had been scheduled to give on September 11, 2001. She discussed the development and education of young children. "Since September 11, I have traveled across the country meeting children and their parents," she said. "As a result, I am doubly committed to using my voice to help give our youngest Americans a real chance to succeed in the classroom, in the university, and in the work place."[1]

On January 28, 2002, Laura Bush and Supreme

Court Justice Anthony Kennedy met with Washington, D.C., high school students for a "Dialogue on Freedom," sponsored by the American Bar Association (ABA). The event gave students the chance to talk about American civic values and the universal rights of all people. The students discussed the concepts of democracy and freedom. Laura Bush told the students that the September 11 attacks "gave us a chance to reassess what our country stands for, what our freedom means and what our responsibilities are as citizens."[2] The ABA, a professional organization for lawyers, continued the program in cities around the nation.

As part of her Ready to Read, Ready to Learn education program, Laura Bush hosted a White House Conference called "Preparing Tomorrow's Teachers" on March 5, 2002. The conference brought together experts in the field of education to discuss ways to improve teacher training. "Our obligation to America's teachers is as clear and strong as our obligation to America's children," she said. "Teachers deserve all the knowledge and support we can give them. And children deserve the quality education that comes from excellent teachers."[3]

Laura Bush also supported efforts to improve the lives of women around the world. On March 8, 2002, she spoke to the United Nations as part of the International Women's Day celebration. She talked

As part of her effort to help women around the world, Laura Bush has hosted discussions on global women's issues.

about the women and children of Afghanistan and how, with help from the United States, their lives had improved. She pointed out how children were able to go to school, many for the first time. "Today, on International Women's Day, we affirm our mission to protect human rights for women in Afghanistan and around the world," she said.[4]

In May 2002, First Lady Laura Bush traveled to Europe without her husband. She spoke at an international public conference in Paris, France. "No matter what country you call home, no matter what our differences in culture or custom or faith, one value transcends every border," she said. "All mothers and fathers the world over love their children and want the very best for them."[5] She emphasized the importance of providing a quality education for children around the world. "The most important gift we can give the world's children is the gift most likely to lead to future peace and prosperity—and that is the gift of a good education," she said.[6]

In Budapest, Hungary, Laura Bush attended a forum on women's health and wellness. In Prague, the capital of the Czech Republic, she delivered the first Radio Free Europe address aimed at Afghanistan. Her thirteen-minute speech was translated into Pashto and Dari, two common languages in Afghanistan. She urged women to get involved in forming a new government. "I'm confident Afghanistan can build a future of peace and freedom," she said, "and America will be your friend and partner in achieving it."[7]

On October 12, 2002, Laura Bush hosted the second National Book Festival in Washington, D.C. "Let this festival remind us of the pure joy of the bookworm," she said.[8] More than seventy authors took part in the event. In addition, basketball players from the National Basketball Association and the Women's National Basketball Association, along with Elmo, Clifford the Big Red Dog, and Arthur joined in the fun. Laura Bush attended the festival with Russian first lady Lyudmila Putin. The two book lovers strolled the

Basketball player Jerry Stackhouse of the Washington Wizards helped launch the 2002 National Book Festival.

grounds together and visited with authors. In the children's tent, they listened to author Eric Carle read his picture book *"Slowly, Slowly, Slowly," said the Sloth.*

In February 2003, Laura Bush was named Honorary Ambassador for the United Nations Decade of Literacy. The goal of the Decade of Literacy is to bring greater literacy to all the countries of the world and to ensure that more women and girls are educated. "These are not simply goals for the next decade—these are moral responsibilities every nation must embrace," said Laura Bush.[9]

The first lady often invited authors and scholars to the White House to discuss literature. She planned an evening to celebrate American poets on February 12, 2003. One of the poets she invited, Sam Hamill, felt strongly that the United States should not invade Iraq, as President Bush was threatening to do. Hamill gathered together a collection of antiwar poems and planned to present it to Laura Bush at the White House. Laura Bush canceled the event, saying that "it would be inappropriate to turn what is intended to be a literary event into a political forum."[10] As much as she would have enjoyed a night of poetry, Laura Bush was loyal to her husband and would not do anything that would put him in a bad light.

In March 2003, President Bush informed the American people that he and his security advisers believed Iraq possessed weapons of mass destruction. He declared Iraqi leader Saddam Hussein a threat to American security. On March 17, President Bush gave Saddam Hussein forty-eight hours to leave Iraq. Two days later, on March 19, 2003, U.S. troops invaded Iraq. Laura Bush was against going to war in Iraq. "Laura trusts my judgment and we talked about it some," said George Bush. "But, of course, she didn't want to go to war."[11]

Laura Bush canceled her travel plans and stayed near her husband. With American soldiers fighting in Afghanistan and Iraq, President Bush drew strength from Laura. She helped him remain calm and focused. "Those of us who have known them over the years can look at them and see they are communicating, even when they aren't talking," said one of Laura Bush's childhood friends. "You see them together, and it's like they are reading each other's minds."[12] To help relieve stress, Laura Bush hired a personal trainer and walked three miles a day on a treadmill. She also read mysteries, her favorite type of book for pure enjoyment.

On May 1, 2003, President Bush announced that major combat operations in Iraq had ended. Laura Bush resumed her travel schedule. She began a program called Preserve America, designed to honor and maintain historic places around the country. Preserve America encouraged an appreciation of America's heritage, from monuments and buildings to landscapes and main streets. She also began campaigning for her husband, who was running for reelection.

Laura Bush played a key role in President Bush's 2004 reelection campaign. She promoted her literacy programs while she campaigned. She also talked about heart disease in women and women's rights as she traveled around the country. President Bush's campaign team recognized Laura Bush's popularity and her importance to the campaign. "She's the kind of woman most Americans admire tremendously," said public opinion expert Whit Ayres. "She's poised. She's cool. She's smart. And you sense a feistiness just beneath the surface."[13]

When Laura Bush entered a room to speak,

audiences cheered. She told voters that she knew George W. Bush better than anyone else and could offer a true picture of what he was really like. President Bush often talked about Laura on the campaign trail. "A good reason to put me back in office is to make sure Laura has four more years as the First Lady," he said.[14]

Barbara and Jenna Bush also campaigned for their father. They worked in his Arlington, Virginia, campaign headquarters and traveled with Laura and George Bush on campaign trips. The twins appeared in a seven-page interview and photo spread in the August 2004 issue of *Vogue* magazine. They spoke at the Republican National Convention at Madison Square Garden in New York City in August 2004. "Jenna and

Barbara, left, and Jenna Bush worked on their father's reelection campaign.

I are really not very political," said Barbara Bush, "but we love our Dad too much to stand back and watch from the sidelines. Besides, since we've graduated from college, we're looking around for something to do for the next few years . . . kind of like Dad."[15]

George W. Bush won the election on November 2, 2004, against Democratic candidate John Kerry. "She's the reason I won," George said of Laura.[16] As Laura Bush helped plan the inauguration, many people criticized the Bush administration. They thought it was extravagant to spend $40 million on a ceremony when American soldiers still occupied Iraq and Afghanistan. Laura Bush insisted that in times of war, the nation's ceremonies should continue. "They're a ritual of our government," she said. "And I think it's really important to have the inauguration every time."[17]

The inauguration was held as planned. Laura Bush wore a white embroidered coat and matching dress for the swearing-in ceremony. She wore an Oscar de la Renta silver and ice-blue gown for the inaugural balls.

With the election behind her, Laura Bush turned her attention to helping America's boys. "We paid a lot of attention to girls over the last 20 or 30 years, but we thought our boys could take care of themselves," she said. "We've come to find out boys need nurturing just like girls do."[18] She started an education program called Helping America's Youth. The goal of the program was to keep at-risk middle and high school boys out of gangs and in school. In his State of the Union address, President Bush said, "Taking on gang life will be one part of a broader outreach to at-risk youth, which involves par-

> **She started Helping America's Youth to keep at-risk boys out of gangs and in school.**

ents and pastors, coaches and community leaders, in programs ranging from literacy to sports. And I am proud that the leader of this nationwide effort will be our First Lady, Laura Bush."[19]

One of Laura Bush's goals for the program was to bring attention to the needs of adolescent boys. "I want to get people to think about how we treat boys," she said. "To some extent they aren't being taught the life skills that we teach girls."[20] She began planning a youth conference to bring child development experts and researchers together to talk about the challenges facing America's young people. She traveled around the United States and visited programs that were working to help at-risk teenagers, especially boys, reach their potential.

In March 2005, under heavy security, Laura Bush traveled to Kabul, Afghanistan. She met with Afghan president Hamid Karzai. They discussed women's rights and educational opportunities for the women of Afghanistan. She visited the Women's Teacher Training Institute. The school provided Afghan women a safe place to be trained as teachers. She announced a multimillion-dollar U.S. grant to help build the American University of Afghanistan. She ate dinner with U.S. troops at Bagram Air Base and thanked them for their service.

The following month, Laura Bush revealed her sense of humor at the White House Correspondents' Association dinner. She poked fun at her husband saying, "George and I were just meant to be. I was the librarian who spent 12 hours a day in the library, yet somehow I met George."[21] She also teased that one of the many differences between her and her husband was that she could pronounce the word "nuclear." (President Bush incorrectly pronounces it "nucular.") The audience of three thousand gave her a standing ovation.

In May, Laura Bush traveled to Jordan to deliver a speech on democracy at the World Economic Forum. "All people—men and women—want to contribute to the success of their country," she said. "And all people—men and women—must have the opportunity to do so."[22] She urged nations to make the education of all its citizens a priority and to make women equal partners with men in exercising freedom. She also visited Muslim, Jewish, and Christian holy sites.

Laura Bush and her daughters traveled to Africa in June 2005 on a goodwill mission. As she sat in a Rwandan church and listened to a speech about the

AIDS epidemic in Africa, Laura Bush noticed a toddler wandering between the pews. When the boy, an orphan with AIDS, stopped beside her, Laura Bush scooped him up and held him on her lap.

Laura Bush and daughter Barbara prayed with HIV-positive mothers in Gwagwalada, Nigeria, in January 2006.

In addition to her international travel, Laura Bush made several trips to the Gulf Coast to reassure and encourage the thousands of people affected by hurricanes Katrina and Rita in 2005.

She also hosted the White House Conference on Helping America's Youth. "Today's Conference . . . is about helping all young people—boys and girls, children and teens—grow up to be healthy and successful adults," she said.[23]

Laura Bush never expected a life in the limelight.

"Choose a Woman, Please"

Laura Bush tries very hard to keep her policy disagreements with her husband private. However, she has her own opinions. For example, when Sandra Day O'Connor announced her retirement from the Supreme Court in the summer of 2005, Laura Bush said from South Africa in an interview for the *Today* show, "I would really like for him to name another woman."[24] President Bush seemed surprised by the public comment. "I didn't realize she'd put this advice in the press," he said. "I can't wait to hear her advice . . . when she gets back."[25]

Reserved by nature, she prefers to work behind the scenes. She never even wanted to speak in public. But despite her plans, this small-town West Texas woman has grown into a popular and dynamic international figure. According to many opinion polls, most Americans, even people who oppose her husband, approve of the way she handles the job of first lady. She travels around the world and shares her love of literature. She promotes a variety of programs designed to make the world a better place. Laura Bush has met each new challenge with grace and poise.

When her term as first lady ends, Laura Bush plans to return to Texas. She will continue to support her husband in whatever he chooses to do. She believes "education opens the door of hope to all the world's children."[26] So, wherever her future takes her, she will continue to promote reading and literacy, her lifelong passions. She also intends to travel, work in the garden, and read stacks of good books. And she will spend lots of time with the most important people in her life: her family and her friends.

Laura Bush is ready for whatever challenges the future holds.

CHRONOLOGY

1946   Laura Welch is born on November 4 in Midland, Texas.

1962   Travels to Monterrey, Mexico, and studies Spanish language and culture.

1964   Graduates from Robert E. Lee High School in Midland.

1968   Graduates from Southern Methodist University with a bachelor's degree in elementary education. Travels to Europe. Begins teaching third grade in Dallas, Texas.

1969   Moves to Houston, Texas, and teaches second grade.

1971   Enrolls at the University of Texas in Austin to study library science.

1973   Graduates with a master's degree in library science. Moves to Houston and works as a children's librarian.

1974   Moves to Austin and works as an elementary-school librarian.

1977   Marries George W. Bush on November 5. Moves back to Midland.

1978   Campaigns with her husband for Congress.

Watches father-in-law, George H.W. Bush, **1981**
sworn in as vice president of the United States in
Washington, D.C. Gives birth to twins, Barbara
and Jenna.

Moves to Washington, D.C., so George W. Bush **1987**
can work on his father's presidential campaign.

Watches George H.W. Bush sworn in as **1989**
president of the United States. Moves to Dallas,
Texas. George W. Bush purchases the Texas
Rangers baseball team.

George W. Bush wins election as governor **1994**
of Texas.

Becomes first lady of Texas. Begins promoting **1995**
reading and literacy in Texas.

Creates the First Lady's Family Literacy Initiative **1996**
for Texas. Organizes the first Texas Book Festival.
Gives a speech at the Republican National
Convention in San Diego, California.

Campaigns for Governor George W. Bush's **1998**
reelection campaign.

Helps write Senate Bill 955 to set aside more **1999**
than $215 million for reading programs in Texas.

Campaigns for George W. Bush for president. **2000**
Speaks at the Republican National Convention
in Philadelphia, Pennsylvania.

2001 Becomes America's first lady. Launches the Ready to Read, Ready to Learn education program. Hosts first National Book Festival in Washington, D.C. Gives presidential radio address.

2002 Testifies before the Senate Education Committee. Hosts a White House Conference, "Preparing Tomorrow's Teachers." Speaks to the United Nations about women's rights. Travels to Europe on first solo trip as first lady.

2003 Named Honorary Ambassador for the United Nations Decade of Literacy. Launches Preserve America to preserve historic places.

2004 Campaigns for George W. Bush for reelection for president. Promotes her Ready to Read, Ready to Learn education program.

2005 Launches nationwide program, Helping America's Youth. Travels to Kabul, Afghanistan, to promote women's rights. Travels to Jordan for the World Economic Forum. Travels to Africa on a goodwill mission.

2006 Travels to Nigeria as Honorary Ambassador of the United Nations Decade for Literacy. Travels to Italy to promote breast cancer awareness and attends the Olympic Games. Works to increase awareness of heart disease in women through the Heart Truth campaign.

LAURA BUSH'S FAVORITE CHILDREN'S BOOKS
A Selected List

Family Reading

Charlotte's Web, E. B. White

Hank the Cowdog series, John R. Erickson

Little House on the Prairie series, Laura Ingalls Wilder

Where the Red Fern Grows, Wilson Rawls

Winnie the Pooh series, A. A. Milne

Books for Young Children

Goodnight Moon, Margaret Wise Brown

Hop on Pop, and others, Dr. Seuss

Where the Wild Things Are, Maurice Sendak

Cars and Trucks and Things that Go, Richard Scarry

Frog and Toad series, Arnold Lobel

If You Give a Pig a Pancake, Laura Joffee Numeroff

Books for Intermediate and Independent Readers

A Year Down Yonder, Richard Peck

Because of Winn Dixie, Kate DiCamillo

Bridge to Terabithia, Katherine Paterson

Where the Sidewalk Ends, Shel Silverstein

Sarah, Plain and Tall, Patricia Maclachlan

Ramona series, Beverly Cleary

CHAPTER NOTES

Chapter 1. The National Book Festival

1. Gail Fineberg, "The Joy of the Written Word," *Library of Congress Information Bulletin*, October 2001, p. 218.

2. Ibid.

3. Craig D'Ooge, "Librarian of Congress and First Lady Launch National Book Festival," *Library of Congress Press Release, 01-107*, July 30, 2001.

4. Fineberg, p. 219.

5. Ibid.

6. Laura Bush, "Remarks by Mrs. Bush at the Book Festival Gala," *Office of Mrs. Bush*, September 7, 2001.

Chapter 2. West Texas Girl

1. Christopher Anderson, *George and Laura: Portrait of an American Marriage* (New York: Avon Books, 2002), p. 96.

2. Julia Reed, "First in Command," *Vogue*, June 2001, p. 219.

3. Georgia Temple, "Childhood Friends Say Laura Bush Loved Books, Scouting," *Midland Reporter-Telegram Supplement*, July 2000, p. 9.

4. Georgia Temple, "Jenna Welch 'Extremely Proud' of Potential First Lady," *Midland Reporter-Telegram Supplement*, July 2000, p. 11.

5. Frank Bruni, "For Laura Bush, a Direction She Never Wished to Go In," *The New York Times*, July 31, 2000.

6. Carolyn Barta, "Laura Bush Accepts SMU Award," *The Dallas Morning News*, October 29, 1999.

7. Georgia Temple, "Journalist Recalls Childhood Memories of Laura Bush," *Midland Reporter-Telegram Supplement*, July 2000, p. 15.

8. Anderson, p. 103.

9. Temple, "Childhood Friends Say Laura Bush Loved Books, Scouting," p. 9.

10. Ibid.

11. Anderson, p. 109.

12. Oprah Winfrey, "Oprah Talks to Laura Bush," *O, The Oprah Magazine*, May 2001, p. 274.

Chapter 3. Teacher and Librarian

1. Lloyd Grove, "Mrs. Bush Goes to Washington," *Harper's Bazaar*, June 2001, p. 161.

2. Family Education Network, "Family Education Network Interview With Laura Bush," July 31, 1999, <http://www. teachervision.fen. com/page/3219.html?detoured=1>, (March 23, 2005).

3. Susan Schindehette, "The First Lady Next Door," *People* magazine, January 29, 2001, p. 56.

4. Ibid.

5. Christopher Anderson, *George and Laura: Portrait of an American Marriage* (New York: Avon Books, 2002), p. 115.

6. Frank Bruni, "For Laura Bush, a Direction She Never Wished to Go In," *The New York Times*, July 31, 2000.

7. Anderson, p. 116.

8. Lois Romano, "Laura Bush: A Twist on Traditional," *Washington Post*, May 14, 2000.

9. "Laura Bush," *MSNBC Headliners and Legends*, January 15, 2005.

10. Schindehette, p. 56.

11. Claudia Feldman, "First Lady," *Houston Chronicle: Texas Magazine*, July 20, 1997, p. 9.

12. Laura Bush, "Opening Remarks by Mrs. Bush at White House Conference on Preparing Tomorrow's Teachers," *Office of Mrs. Bush*, March 5, 2002.

13. Laurence McQuillan, "Laura Bush's Travel Agenda: Education," *USA Today*, March 22, 2001.

14. Nancy Bilyeau, "Meet the Next First Lady," *Good Housekeeping*, October 2000, p. 166.

Chapter 4. A Perfect Match

1. Claudia Feldman, "First Lady," *Houston Chronicle: Texas Magazine*, July 20, 1997, p. 9.

2. Ibid.

3. Skip Hollandsworth, "Younger. Wilder?" *Texas Monthly*, June 1999, p. 143.

4. Kimberly Goad, "Laura Bush: Adjusting to the Spotlight, the First Lady Relishes Her New Role," *The Dallas Morning News*, September 24, 1995.

5. Skip Hollandsworth, "Reading Laura Bush," *Texas Monthly*, November 1996, p. 152.

6. George W. Bush, *A Charge to Keep* (New York: William Morrow and Company, Inc., 1999), p. 79.

7. Nancy Bilyeau, "Meet the Next First Lady," *Good Housekeeping*, October 2000, p. 166.

8. Bill Minutaglio, *First Son: George W. Bush and the Bush Family Dynasty* (New York: Three Rivers Press, 1999), p. 185.

9. Skip Hollandsworth, "Born to Run: What's in a Name?" *Texas Monthly*, May 1994, p. 148.

10. Lloyd Grove, "Mrs. Bush Goes to Washington," *Harper's Bazaar*, June 2001, p. 186.

11. Saeed Ahmed and Julie Bonnin, "Speech May Shed Light on Reticent Half of Texas' First Couple," *The Atlanta Journal-Constitution*, July 30, 2000.

12. Grove, p. 186.

13. Christopher Anderson, *George and Laura: Portrait of an American Marriage* (New York: Avon Books, 2002), p. 149.

14. Minutaglio, p. 186.

15. Anderson, p. 152.

16. Ellen Levine, "We Are All Changed. Every One of Us Has Changed." *Good Housekeeping*, January 2002, p. 150.

17. Hollandsworth, "Reading Laura Bush," p. 120.

18. Julie Bonnin, "What Laura Wants," *The Austin American-Statesman*, April 18, 1999.

19. "Laura Bush," *MSNBC Headliners and Legends*, January 15, 2005.

20. Diane Reischel, "George W. Bush: Politics, Baseball and Life in the Shadow of the White House," *The Dallas Morning News*, February 25, 1990.

21. Anderson, p. 156.

Chapter 5. Babies and Baseball

1. Oprah Winfrey, "Oprah Talks to Laura Bush," *O, The Oprah Magazine*, May 2001, p. 270.

2. George W. Bush, *A Charge to Keep* (New York: William Morrow and Company, Inc., 1999), p. 84.

3. George W. Bush, "Presidential Candidate George Bush," *The Oprah Winfrey Show* transcript, September 19, 2000, p. 17.

4. Christopher Anderson, *George and Laura: Portrait of an American Marriage* (New York: Avon Books, 2002), p. 163.

5. Bush, *A Charge to Keep*, p. 85.

6. Laura Bush, "National Federation of Republican Women's Tribute to Laura Bush," *FDCH Political Transcripts*, August 3, 2000.

7. Winfrey, "Oprah Talks to Laura Bush," p. 270.

8. Paul Burka, "The Education of Laura Bush," *Texas Monthly*, April 2001, p. 124.

9. Julie Bonnin, "What Laura Wants," *The Austin American-Statesman*, April 18, 1999.

10. "Laura Bush." *MSNBC Headliners and Legends*, January 15, 2005.

11. Claudia Feldman, "First Lady," *Houston Chronicle: Texas Magazine*, July 20, 1997, p. 14.

12. Julia Reed, "First in Command," *Vogue*, June 2001, p. 223.

13. Antonia Felix, *Laura: America's First Lady, First Mother* (Avon, Mass.: Adams Media Corporation, 2002), p. 92.

14. Anderson, p. 204.

Chapter 6. First Lady of Texas

1. Christopher Anderson, *George and Laura: Portrait of an American Marriage* (New York: Avon Books, 2002), p. 213.

2. Kimberly Goad, "Laura Bush: Adjusting to the Spotlight, the First Lady Relishes Her New Role," *The Dallas Morning News*, September 24, 1995.

3. Gregory Curtis, "At Home With Laura," *Time*, January 8, 2001, p. 32.

4. Judy Woodruff, "Laura Bush on Her First Six Months in the White House." *CNN TV* transcript, July 31, 2001, p. 7.

5. Skip Hollandsworth, "Reading Laura Bush," *Texas Monthly*, November 1996, p. 153.

6. Goad, "Laura Bush."

7. Laura Bush, "Text of Remarks by George W. Bush, Governor of Texas, and Laura Bush." *Republican National Convention*, San Diego, August 12, 1996.

8. Hollandsworth, p. 154.

9. Claudia Feldman, "First Lady," *Houston Chronicle: Texas Magazine*, July 20, 1997, p. 11.

10. "Texas Public Libraries to Receive $300,000 From Texas Book Festival," *Texas State Library and Archives Commission*, January 4, 2000.

11. Goad, "Laura Bush."

12. Julia Reed, "First in Command," *Vogue*, June 2001, p. 219.

13. George W. Bush, *A Charge to Keep* (New York: William Morrow and Company, Inc., 1999), p. 93.

14. Bush, *A Charge to Keep*, p. 94.

15. Elaine Sciolino, "Laura Bush Sees Everything in Its Place, Including Herself," *The New York Times*, January 15, 2001.

Chapter 7. Election 2000

1. Paul Burka, "The Education of Laura Bush," *Texas Monthly*, April 2001, p. 124.

2. Julie Bonnin, "What Laura Wants," *The Austin American-Statesman*, April 18, 1999.

3. Frank Bruni, "For Laura Bush, a Direction She Never Wished to Go In," *The New York Times*, July 31, 2000.

4. "Laura Bush," *MSNBC Headliners and Legends*, January 15, 2005.

5. George W. Bush, "George W. and Laura Bush Discuss Election 2000." *CNN Larry King Live* transcript, July 20, 2000, p. 6.

6. Martha Brant, "Don't Call Her an 'Adviser,'" *Newsweek*, August 7, 2000, p. 40.

7. Ibid.

8. Julia Reed, "The Calm Amid the Storm," *Newsweek*, November 22, 1999, p. 43.

9. The News Hour With Jim Lehrer, "Republican Convention 2000 Video/Audio," <http://www.pbs.org/newshour/election2000/gopconvention/video-night1.html> (March 23, 2005).

10. Laura Bush, "Address to the Republican National Convention: Education and Responsibility," Delivered to the Republican National Convention, Philadelphia, Pennsylvania, July 31, 2000, Vital Speeches of the Day, August 15, 2000.

11. Ibid.

12. Myrna Blyth and Nancy Evans, "Fighting for the Family," *Ladies' Home Journal*, November 2000, p. 138.

13. John Hanchette, "Laura Bush, Librarian and Teacher, Has Become Formidable Campaigner," *The Seattle Times*, June 26, 2000.

14. Paul Burka, "The Education of Laura Bush," *Texas Monthly*, April 2001, p. 122.

15. Ellen Levine, "We Are All Changed. Every One of Us Has Changed," *Good Housekeeping*, January 2002, p. 103.

16. John Hanchette, "Laura Welch Bush: Shy No More," *USA Today*, June 23, 2000.

17. Nicholas D. Kristof, "How Bush Came to Tame His Inner Scamp," *The New York Times*, July 29, 2000.

18. Lois Romano, "Laura Bush: A Twist on Traditional," *Washington Post*, May 14, 2000.

19. Michael Corcoran, "Texas Book Festival Gala Loaded With Election Jokes," *The Austin American-Statesman*, November 11, 2000.

20. Carolyn Barta, "Learning to Like the Limelight: Laura Bush Growing Into Possible Role as President's First Lady," *The Dallas Morning News*, July 30, 2000.

21. Christopher Anderson, *George and Laura: Portrait of an American Marriage* (New York: Avon Books, 2002), p. 283.

Chapter 8. America's First Lady

1. Michael Kilian, "Bush Family Comes Back to Town, and Laura Bush Put on Pedestal," *Chicago Tribune*, January 19, 2001.

2. Ann Gerhart, *The Perfect Wife: The Life and Choices of Laura Bush* (New York: Simon & Schuster, 2004), p. 118.

3. Sharon Jayson, "A Literary Introduction: Laura Bush Honors America's Authors in Washington Debut," *The Austin American-Statesman*, January 20, 2001.

4. Ellen Levine, "'We Are All Changed. Every One Of Us Has Changed,'" *Good Housekeeping*, January 2002, p. 103.

5. "The 50 Most Beautiful People in the World 2001: Laura Bush," *People*, May 14, 2001, p. 160.

6. Oprah Winfrey, "Oprah Talks to Laura Bush." *O, The Oprah Magazine*, May 2001, p. 204.

7. Jena Heath, "Laura, As First Lady, Remains 'Just Like You and Me,'" *The Austin American-Statesman*, June 10, 2001.

8. Gerhart, p. 131.

9. Saeed Ahmed and Julie Bonnin, "Speech May Shed Light on Reticent Half of Texas' First Couple," *The Atlanta Journal-Constitution*, July 30, 2000.

10. Elaine Sciolino, "Laura Bush Sees Everything in Its Place, Including Herself," *The New York Times*, January 15, 2001.

11. "The 50 Most Beautiful People in the World 2001: Laura Bush," p. 160.

12. Ibid.

13. Christopher Anderson, *George and Laura: Portrait of an American Marriage* (New York: Avon Books, 2002), p. 303.

14. Gerhart, p. 128.

15. Laura Bush, "Remarks of Laura Bush at the White House Summit on Early Childhood Cognitive Development," *White House Summit on Early Childhood Development*, Washington, D.C., July 26, 2001.

16. Craig D'Ooge, "Librarian of Congress and First Lady Launch National Book Festival," *Library of Congress Press Release, 01-107*, July 30, 2001.

17. Laura Bush, "Mrs. Bush Announces Creation of Laura Bush Foundation For America's Libraries," July 30, 2001, <http://www.laurabushfoundation.org/release.html> (November 29, 2004).

18. James A. Barnes, "The Un-Hillary," *National Journal*, April 28, 2001, p. 1259.

Chapter 9. Comforter-in-Chief

1. Laura Bush, "Remarks by Mrs. Bush at the National Press Club," *Office of Mrs. Bush*, November 8, 2001.

2. Ann Gerhart, *The Perfect Wife: The Life and Choices of Laura Bush* (New York: Simon & Schuster, 2004), p. 162.

3. Ann Gerhart, "Laura Bush, Comforter In Chief," *The Washington Post*, September 19, 2001.

4. Laura Bush, "Remarks by Mrs. Bush at the National Press Club."

5. Laura Bush, "How to Talk to Children About America Under Attack." *The Oprah Winfrey Show* transcript, September 18, 2001, p. 3.

6. Bob Woodward, *Bush At War* (New York: Simon & Schuster, 2002), p. 28.

7. George W. Bush, "Remarks by the President in Photo Opportunity With the National Security Team," *Office of President George W. Bush*, September 12, 2001.

8. "All Necessary And Appropriate Force," *CBS News.com*, September 13, 2001, <http://www.cbsnews.com/stories/2001/09/14/attack/printable311312.shtml> (April 12, 2005).

9. George W. Bush, "Guard and Reserves Define Spirit of America: Remarks by the President to Employees at the Pentagon," *Office of President George W. Bush*, September 17, 2001.

10. Woodward, p. 101.

11. Ken Herman, "Laura Bush: First Lady Stays Calm and Strong During National Tragedy," *The Austin American-Statesman*, September 20, 2001.

12. Laura Bush, "Elementary School Letter," *Office of Mrs. Bush*, September 12, 2001.

13. Laura Bush, "Remarks by Mrs. Bush at Memorial Service in Pennsylvania," *Office of Mrs. Bush*, September 17, 2001.

14. Gerhart, "Laura Bush, Comforter In Chief."

15. Laura Bush, "How to Talk to Children About America Under Attack," p. 18.

16. Deborah Orin, "Laura Truly Our First Mom Sees Role As Calming Influence," *The New York Post*, September 23, 2001, p. 10.

17. Larry King, "Interview With Laura Bush," *CNN Larry King Live* transcript, December 18, 2001, p. 1.

18. Woodward, p. 171.

19. Ellen Levine, "We Are All Changed. Every One of Us Has Changed," *Good Housekeeping*, January 2002, p. 102.

20. Kati Marton, "A New Chapter for Laura Bush," *Newsweek*, October 8, 2001, p. 33.

21. Laura Bush, "Remarks by Mrs. Bush at the National Press Club."

22. Herman, "Laura Bush: First Lady Stays Calm and Strong During National Tragedy."

23. Laura Bush, "Radio Address by Mrs. Bush," *Office of Mrs. Bush*, November 17, 2001.

24. Larry King, "America's New War: Laura Bush Discusses the Impact of September 11," *CNN Larry King Live* transcript, October 2, 2001, p. 3.

Chapter 10. On the World Stage

1. Laura Bush, "Mrs. Bush's Remarks Before the Senate Committee on Health, Education, Labor and Pensions," *Office of Mrs. Bush*, January 24, 2002.

2. Jan Crawford Greenburg, "Justice Kennedy, Laura Bush Engage Students in 'Dialogue on Freedom,'" *Chicago Tribune*, January 28, 2002.

3. Laura Bush, "Opening Remarks by Mrs. Bush at White House Conference on Preparing Tomorrow's Teachers," *Office of Mrs. Bush*, March 5, 2002.

4. Laura Bush, "Remarks by Mrs. Bush to the United Nations," *Office of Mrs. Bush*, March 8, 2002.

5. Laura Bush, "Remarks by Mrs. Bush at Organization for Economic Cooperation and Development (OECD) Forum," *Office of Mrs. Bush*, May 14, 2002.

6. Ibid.

7. Laura Bush, "Radio Address of First Lady Laura Bush to Radio Free Afghanistan," *Office of Mrs. Bush*, May 21, 2002.

8. Michael Kilian, "Writers, Readers, Laura Bush Celebrate the Joy of Books," *Chicago Tribune*, October 18, 2002.

9. Laura Bush, "Remarks by Mrs. Bush at UNESCO—Decade of Literacy," *Office of Mrs. Bush*, February 13, 2003.

10. Elisabeth Bumiller, "With Antiwar Poetry Set, Mrs. Bush Postpones Event," *The New York Times*, January 30, 2003.

11. Bob Woodward, *Plan of Attack* (New York: Simon & Schuster, 2004), p. 244.

12. Susan Schindehette, "What a Difference a Year Makes," *People*, January 21, 2002, p. 87.

13. Andrea Stone, "Laura Bush Testifies to Husband's Leadership," *USA Today*, September 1, 2004.

14. George Bush, "Remarks By President Bush at 2004 RNC Gala." *Republican National Committee*, May 6, 2004.

15. Barbara Bush, "Remarks By Jenna and Barbara Bush at the 2004 Republican National Convention," *Republican National Committee*, September 1, 2004.

16. Julia Reed, "Winning Combination," *Vogue*, January 2005, p. 124.

17. Julie Mason, "Laura Bush Insists the Inauguration Must Go On," *Houston Chronicle*, January 15, 2005.

18. Martha Nelson and Sandra Sobieraj Westfall, "A Winning Season," *People*, December 27, 2004, p. 88.

19. George W. Bush, "State of the Union Address," *Office of President George W. Bush*, February 2, 2005.

20. Jeanne Marie Laskas, "The Most Important Part Is Love," *Ladies' Home Journal*, May 2005, p. 170.

21. Mark Silva, "First Lady Stands Out With Stand-Up," *Houston Chronicle*, May 2, 2005.

22. Laura Bush, "Mrs. Bush Delivers Remarks at the World Economic Forum," *Office of the First Lady*, May 21, 2005.

23. Laura Bush, "President and Mrs. Bush Discuss Helping America's Youth at White House Conference," *Office of the Press Secretary*, October 27, 2005.

24. Kathy Kiely, "Bush Gets Court Advice, Some Unexpected," *USA Today*, July 13, 2005.

25. Ibid.

26. Laura Bush, "Remarks by Mrs. Bush at Organization for Economic Cooperation and Development (OECD) Forum," *Office of Mrs. Bush*, May 14, 2002.

FURTHER READING

Gormley, Beatrice. *Laura Bush: America's First Lady*. New York: Aladdin Paperbacks, 2003.

Marquez, Heron. *George W. Bush*. Minneapolis, Minn.: Lerner Publications, 2001.

Pastan, Amy. *First Ladies*. New York: Dorling Kindersley, 2001.

Stone, Tanya Lee. *Laura Welch Bush: First Lady*. Brookfield, Conn.: Millbrook Press, 2001.

Wade, Mary Dodson. *George W. Bush: Governor of Texas*. Austin, Tex.: W. S. Benson & Company, Inc., 1999.

Watson, Robert P. *First Ladies of the United States: A Biographical Dictionary*. Boulder, Colo.: Lynne Rienner Publishers, Inc., 2001.

INTERNET ADDRESSES

Official White House Web site for the first lady
<http://www.whitehouse.gov/firstlady>

Laura Bush's foundation for helping America's libraries
<http://www.laurabushfoundation.org>

Information on how you can get involved in your community to help America's youth
<http://www.helpingamericasyouth.gov>

INDEX

Page numbers for photographs are in **boldface** type.

NEW YORK MILLS
PUBLIC LIBRARY
399 MAIN STREET
N.Y. MILLS, NY 13417